How A Reel Repair Business

"Service through Excellence"

Piscator Publishing – Los Angeles, California
©2009

Copyright 2009 Jeff Holder. Printed and bound in the United States of America. All rights reserved. No part of this book may be reproduced or transmitted in any form or by any means, electronic or mechanical, including photocopying, recording, or by an information storage and retrieval system – with the exception of a reviewer who may quote brief passages in a review to be printed in a newspaper or magazine – without written permission from the publisher or author. For information contact jeff@reelschematic.com

This book includes information from many sources and gathered from many personal experiences. It is published for general reference and is not intended to be substitute for independent verification by readers when necessary and appropriate. The book is sold with the understanding that neither the author nor the publisher is engaged in rendering financial or legal advice. The publisher and author disclaim any personal liability, directly or indirectly, for advice or information presented within. Although the author and publisher have prepared this manuscript with utmost care and diligence and have made every effort to ensure the accuracy and completeness of the information contained within, we assume no responsibility for errors, inaccuracies, omissions, or inconsistencies.

DEDICATION

This book is dedicated to my wife Kathleen, my children Haley, Candice, Cassie and Aaron. Thanks to my father for the many fishing trips during my youth and to my mother, god bless her. All of whom this book would never have been possible.

Foreword

My goal is to teach you what is involved in starting your own reel repair business. The fact is starting any business can be scary and full of pitfalls for the uninformed entrepreneur; thankfully you have taken the right step to making your business a success by purchasing this book!

While it doesn't take a genius to open a store and place a welcome sign in the window, it does take some understanding of business practices, marketing and sales in order to separate your business from the pack and make it successful. I have taken several businesses, including ReelSchematic from just an idea to a now worldwide recognized leader in fishing reel resources. In this book I am going to share with you the secrets of my success and how you can use the exact same techniques to build your business with very little money.

Not everything works the same for every business, and all things are not always cut and dry but these simple steps worked for me and they can also work for you. I have founded and owned both brick and mortar retail stores as well as online businesses, both which require different marketing strategies, and will be discussed further in the book. I have authored another best-selling book among anglers entitled "Fishing Reel Care and Maintenance 101" which is the first book to ever focus primarily on fishing reels and how to properly maintain and repair them. Obviously if you purchased this book you are serious about starting your own business, my first recommendation is that you purchase "Fishing Reel Care and Maintenance 101" which includes valuable information you can use on a daily basis for your new business which is not covered in depth in this book.

I have fished and repaired reels since I was old enough to hold a pole in my hand almost four decades ago. Fishing reels have gone through many technological advances over that period of time and as a Reel Repair business owner you will be dealing with many different models, years and brands of reels. All of which you have to treat with equal care and priority, if a customer brings a reel into your shop no matter the brand, age, or model, that reel means something to the angler and if you treat their reel with the utmost care they expect then you will gain a loyal customer.

When I started my first business I knew very little about what I was getting into and believe me when I say I made my share of mistakes. I am going to teach you ways to avoid making those same mistakes and the right things you need to do to get your reel repair business on the fast track to success.

I will touch on the subject of reel repairing and servicing but this book is mainly about your reel repair business and getting it off the ground and keeping it off the ground, if you want to learn more specifics on reel repair you need my other book "Fishing Reel Care and Maintenance 101".

Table of Contents

WHERE TO START
- Leap of Faith 1
- Home Office or Leased Property 2

DOING BUSINESS 6
- What's In A Name 7
- Fictitious Business Name 11
- Federal Tax Identification Number 13
- Sales Tax and Business Licenses 20
- Bank Accounts and Credit Cards 21
- Accountants, CPA's 24

LET'S GET STARTED
- What You Need To Get Started 28
- Tools and Equipment 31
- Pricing Your Services 32
- Employees 35
- Customer Records 36
- Vendor Records 38

DESIGNING YOUR WEBSITE
- Your Online Presence 41
  - Domain Name and Hosting 45
  - Your Business Email 47
  - Solid Foundation 48
  - META Tags 50
  - Image Tags and Link Titles 53
  - Search Engine Optimization Tips 54

REEL MAINTENANCE
- Reel Repair Pickup Locations 71

MARKETING AND ADVERTISING
    Conventional Advertising 74
    Email Marketing 75
    Google Adwords 78
    Advertising On Other Sites 81

COMPETITORS
    How to handle them 86

SAMPLE FORMS
    Reel Service Drop-off 90
    Reel Service Price List 92

REEL SERVICE AND PARTS DIRECTORY 93

REEL WARRANTY SERVICE
    Abu-Garcia Reels 96
    Accurate Reels 96
    Avet Reels 100
    Daiwa Reels 102
    Fin-Nor Reels 104
    Hardy Reels 107
    Okuma Reels 108
    Pinnacle Reels 109
    Penn Reels 111
    Quantum Reels 113
    Shakespeare Reels 116
    Shimano Reels 119
    Zebco Reels 120

INDEX 123

WHERE TO START

Leap of Faith

So you've probably been repairing reels for your friends and family, and maybe from time to time they've told you, "Hey you should start your own reel repair business", and so slowly the seed was planted in your head.

Until one day you starting asking yourself, could this be a viable full-time or part-time as a supplemental income. That's could be a loaded question, because "Yes" it definitely can be a viable business and is for thousands of reel repair businesses around the world, will it be for you? That all depends on you, and what you put into it.

Deciding to start your own business is not an easy task and can leave you lying awake at night staring at the ceiling wondering where to start, what you need, what you need in terms of legality and even if you should do it at all.

Fortunately in this business there are some great alternatives that can allow you to test the waters for your new business without putting everything on the line. In fact almost all entrepreneurs start out working part-time while still keeping their full-time jobs to pay the bills, besides we all can't be starving artists can we. If starting your business part-time is the only way you would feel comfortable or the only way that it is financially feasible for you, then you've already made the most important decision. Unless you have a lot of startup capital ($$), and have already built a good following of loyal customers, I would strongly suggest you start out part-time with minimal financial investment.

Now by part-time I don't necessary mean you only work 3-4 hours on weekends, what I mean is start out with a home office, a garage-type work area, and if you are not retired and work a full time job, keep it, at least for now.

Even if you starting up your business part-time at home does not mean that you can make a half hearted commitment. *I will tell you right now unless you are willing to commit yourself 100% to making your business a success then failure is in your path.*

You might find yourself doing less fishing, yes I know it's horrible, weekends and nights the business will sometimes take much of your time, and sometimes holidays as well. But the rewards of owning your business, steering your own course, is worth every second you spend investing your time in your business's future.

Home Office or Leased Property

While both have their advantages, and we will discuss those in this section. For some a home office might be too distracting because of several factors including other family members, and the honey-do list sometimes never seems to end. If you can't find an area, garage, workshop or spare bedroom that you can close the doors to then sometimes the only alternative might be to look for space away from your home. This can mean leasing property.

Leased property can come in many various forms, one in particular that most people don't think about is checking with local area tackle shops that don't currently handle in-house reel repair and making them an offer to give a certain percentage of each repair service taken in by that store in exchange for a working area. You will be surprised how many tackle shops will be glad to have an additional in-house service they can offer their customers and the extra money won't hurt either. This gives you a nice working area, and a convenient place for your customers to drop-off and pick-up their reels.

Cons of leasing a space for your business are:

1. You have signed a legally binding lease contract, for which if your business is not the success you had hoped or unforeseen circumstances arise, it can cost you literally thousands of dollars to terminate the lease.
2. Everything costs more, as a business entity you are charged at a higher rate for phone and Internet access. Why? Because they can.

Pros of leasing a space for your business are:

1. You instantly become a more reputable and reliable business because people like a brick and mortar business, it makes them feel more secure doing business with you.
2. You can get instant foot traffic, especially if you are located in an area with great existing anchor stores. (And not the kind you tie to your boat to hold it steady!)
3. It avoids a lot of mixing business with personal life by separating your business from your home; this will save you time and expense when it comes tax time.
4. It allows you the ability of providing a physical mailing address and phone without sharing your personal home address and personal home phone for business.
5. If you hire employees it is safer by having them at a commercial store than your personal home. Face it; do you want potential strangers working in your home?
6. You can concentrate on running your business without the distractions of home life.

> TIP: If you do your business from home you should get a Post Office Box that you can use for all your business needs.

Since you are just starting out, and you are more than likely the owner and the sole employee at this point, I would recommend a home office or agreed space in a tackle store as discussed earlier.

In another section we will discuss how no matter where you locate your business the number one presence you need is on the Internet. There are an estimated 82 million anglers in the world today and 60% (40.8 million) use the Internet on a daily or weekly basis. The world has changed over the last couple of decades, long gone are the days when your business could only survive if you paid out thousands in marketing in the form of HUGE phone book ads, newspaper or magazine ads, or even billboards. The Internet is "King", and will be your greatest resource for marketing your services.

I don't want to give you false hopes of fortunes, and get rich quick schemes because honestly they do not exist. Your financial rewards will be balanced by how much sweat and time you put into the business. The Internet is not a magical marketing vehicle that will instantly provide you with customers banging at your door; it is simply another vehicle that if used effectively will give you a much broader audience than ever offered in the past to the small business owner.

Doing Business

"A real entrepreneur is somebody who has no safety net underneath them." ~ Henry Kravis

What's in a Name

One of the first steps after you decide to start your new business is deciding on a name for your business. You should pick a name that you will be proud to call your business, something easy for customers to remember, easy to identify with the type of service you are providing. This is called "name recognition".

Stay away from hard to pronounce or spell names, be as simple as you can. There are several reasons for this, one because it will be much easier for your customers to remember, we've all been there when trying to tell someone else about a business and all we can come up with is, "I can't remember the name right now, it start with a C". Secondly, when using it as a domain name for your online site you want it to be simple and easy to remember as well, there is nothing worse than naming your business a long complex name for example www.bobsinhousereelrepairservicecenter.com, trust me no one is going to remember it.

Be sure to check that your business name is available as a website domain name, because you don't want to wait to find out later that the name is already taken on the Internet. Also something to consider, if you use your surname within the name of the business and it does not suggest the existence of additional owners then you do not have to get a fictitious business name, as discussed next.

Also fewer letters in the name will lead to fewer costs when creating business cards, flyers, etc, although minimum savings, it all adds up.

TIP: A great place to check for domain name availability is at www.cheapville.com, I have personally used them on many occasions and have never had an issue.

Be creative, give some time in thinking about the name, and ask friends or family for their input and ideas, you never know they might think of something you didn't. This is not something to rush; after all you will live with the name throughout the course of your business.

TIP: Another point I want to make, after you choose your business name don't decide six months later that you want to rename it to something else, you will destroy your already hard work and name recognition that you have started, not to mention your online presence. This can be a very costly maneuver, both financially and in marketing.

If you plan on having a store front, consider that for signage the cost is by the number of letters in the name, so less is better in this case as well and will save you money.

Think about how will it sound saying the name over and over when you answer the phones, how it looks on letterhead, invoices, receipts, etc.

Whatever you decide to use make sure the name conveys the business, "Reel Service Doctor" conveys exactly what the business is about, however "The

Service Doctor" is very vague and will leave your potential customers guessing. Besides you don't want a bunch of sick people showing up at your door wanting to see the doctor, now do you?

Six things a business name should do

1. *It tells who you are:* Your name should reflect your identity. This is very essential in branding. Since you will be promoting your business name, putting it in the front of as many eyes as possible. How do you want the public to think of you? One successful reel repair shop runs under the business name "The Reel Doctor" because that's how his first customers identified him. I doubt most his customers even know his first name, but everybody in his market knows "The Reel Doctor".
2. *It tells what you do:* I am always amazed at how many business names lend very little to what type of work they actually do. For example, "Bob & Rob", can you tell me what they do? Of course not. That is because they are relying on customers already knowing who they are, and this is very risky for new businesses.
3. *Tells how you do it:* When selecting your business name be careful the words you choose, you can convey a great deal about your company with the name. Consider these names, "Speedy Reel Repair", "Quality Reel

Repair" or "Low-Cost Reel Repair". All three businesses are providing the exact same services, yet each conveys a different message to customers.
4. Separates you from your peers: Your business name is the first opportunity you have to tell customers how you differ from your competitors. You can do this by emphasizing what make your business unique, what services can't be found anywhere else, or how you do it better than anyone else. In the example of the previous three reel repair businesses, each company has a different focus and attracts different types of customers. All this conveyed in less than 4 words.
5. Grab your customer's interest: This aspect is an art form in itself. Think about your target customers, what qualities of your services are the most important to them? "Speedy Reel Repair", will appeal to those anglers that need their reels fast. While "Quality Reel Repair" will appeal more to anglers that care most about the quality of service performed than speed. And even still "Low-Cost Reel Repair" will appeal to anglers with a budget in mind.
6. Make you name approachable: You want your business name to be inviting and approachable as perceived by your target customers. For example, for years Charles Schwab cultivated a classic, formal image.

But now that the consumer base has switched from "old people with money" to "everyone with a 401k", Charles Schwab has launched "Talk to Chuck" in an effort to become more approachable.

Fictitious Business Name (DBA)

A fictitious business name or DBA (short for "doing business as"), allows you to legally do business under a particular name. You can accept payments, advertise, open a bank account, and otherwise present yourself under that name. This is the least expensive way for a sole proprietor to legally do business under a business name without creating a formal legal entity (corporation, partnership, etc.).

If you will be using a fictitious business name, that is the name does not contain any part of your surname, you will have to register it. First let me explain what a fictitious business name is:

FOR INDIVIDUALS OR SOLE PROPRIETORS: A name that does not include the surname of the individual. A name that suggests existence of additional owners (such words as "Company," "& Company," "& Sons," "& Associates," "Brothers;" but not words that merely describe the business being conducted).

FOR PARTNERSHIPS or other association of persons: A name that does not include surname of each general partner or a name that suggests existence of additional owners (such as "Company," "Brothers," etc.). (In the case of an unincorporated association other than a partnership, a "general partner" means a person whose liability in the business is substantially the same as a general partner.)

Recording a fictitious business name is normally done at your County Clerk and Recorder's Office. Fictitious business name filing fees vary county to county, and state to state, but normally cost about $35.00. In some U.S. States filing a fictitious business name is handled at the state level. Check with your state to see how filing is handled and at what level.

There are other laws as well that you will need to be aware of such as some counties require that you register a fictitious business name within 40 days of first transacting business, and most are good for up to 5 years before renewal.

Normally you will be required to publish a fictitious business name statement in one of your local adjudicated newspapers one day per week for four weeks, and must start within 30 days of filing the fictitious business name statement. The cost varies from newspaper to newspaper so it can pay to shop around, and the County Clerk Office can provide you with a list of local newspapers that will publish it for you.

Why are you required to register? Consumer protection laws are require registration because assume for a moment that you are the customer and you are having a disagreement with a business which uses a fictitious business name, without registering there would be no way to find out for lawsuit purposes who the owner is without having to hire a private investigator.

FEDERAL TAX INDENTIFICATION NUMBER (EIN)

An Employer Identification Number (EIN, also known as a Federal Tax Identification Number, is used to identify a business entity. If you will be doing any of the following you will also need to obtain an EIN or better known as a Federal Tax Identification Number.

1. You will have employees, not counting yourself.
2. Operating your business as a corporation or partnership.
3. File any of these tax returns: employment, excise, alcohol, tobacco, or firearms.
4. Withhold taxes on income, other than wages, paid to a non-resident alien.
5. You have a Keogh plan.

You can easily apply online for an EIN at: http://www.irs.gov/businesses/small/article/0,,id=98350,00.html

TIP: Want to search EIN number for a business, here is a great site just for that http://www.einfinder.com/

Sole Proprictors

You **will be** required to obtain a new EIN if any of the following statements are true.

- You are subject to a bankruptcy proceeding.

- You incorporate.
- You take in partners and operate as a partnership.
- You purchase or inherit an existing business that you operate as a sole proprietorship.

You **will not** be required to obtain a new EIN if any of the following statements are true.

- You change the name of your business.
- You change your location and/or add other locations.
- You operate multiple businesses.

Corporations

You **will be** required to obtain a new EIN if any of the following statements are true.

- A corporation receives a new charter from the secretary of state.
- You are a subsidiary of a corporation using the parent's EIN or you become a subsidiary of a corporation.
- You change to a partnership or a sole proprietorship.
- A new corporation is created after a statutory merger.

You **will not** be required to obtain a new EIN if any of the following statements are true.

- You are a division of a corporation.
- The surviving corporation uses the existing EIN after a corporate merger.
- A corporation declares bankruptcy.

- The corporate name or location changes.
- A corporation chooses to be taxed as an S corporation.
- Reorganization of a corporation changes only the identity or place.

Partnerships

You **will be** required to obtain a new EIN if any of the following statements are true.

- You incorporate.
- Your partnership is taken over by one of the partners and is operated as a sole proprietorship.
- You end an old partnership and begin a new one.

You **will not** be required to obtain a new EIN if any of the following statements are true.

- The partnership declares bankruptcy.
- The partnership name changes.
- You change the location of the partnership or add other locations.
- A new partnership is formed as a result of the termination of a partnership under IRC section 708(b)(1)(B).
- 50 percent or more of the ownership of the partnership (measured by interests in capital and profits) changes hands within a twelve-month period (terminated partnerships under Reg. 301.6109-1).

Limited Liability Company (LLC)

An LLC is an entity created by state statute. The IRS did not create a new tax classification for the LLC when it was created by the states; instead IRS uses the tax entity classifications it has always had for business taxpayers: corporation, partnership, or disregarded as an entity separate from its owner, referred to as a "disregarded entity." An LLC is always classified by the IRS as one of these types of taxable entities. If a "disregarded entity" is owned by an individual, it is treated as a sole proprietor. If the "disregarded entity" is owned any any other entity, it is treated as a branch or division of its owner.

Changes affecting Single Member LLCs with Employees

For wages paid on or after January 1, 2009, single member/single owner LLCs that have not elected to be treated as corporations may be required to change the way they report and pay federal employment taxes and wage payments and certain federal excise taxes. On Aug. 16, 2007, changes to Treasury Regulation Section 301.7701-2 were issued. The new regulations state that the LLC, not its single owner, will be responsible for filing and paying all employment taxes on wages paid on or after January 1, 2009. These regulations also state that for certain excise taxes, the LLC, not its single owner, will be responsible for liabilities imposed and actions first required or permitted in periods beginning on or after January 1, 2008.

If a single member LLC has been filing and paying employment taxes under the name and EIN of the owner, and no EIN was previously assigned to the LLC, a new EIN will be required for wages paid on or after January 1, 2009.

If a single member LLC has been filing and paying excise taxes under the name and EIN of the owner and no EIN was previously assigned to the LLC, a new EIN will be required for certain excise tax liabilities imposed and actions first required or permitted in periods beginning on or after January 1, 2008. The following examples may assist in determining if a new EIN is required:

- If the primary name on the account is John Doe, a new EIN will be required.
- If the primary name on the account is John Doe and the second name line is Doe Plumbing (which was organized as an LLC under state law), a new EIN is required.
- If the primary name on the account is Doe Plumbing LLC, a new EIN will not be required.

You **will be** required to obtain a new EIN if any of the following statements are true.

- A new LLC with more than one owner (Multi-member LLC) is formed under state law.
- A new LLC with one owner (Single Member LLC) is formed under state law and chooses to be taxed as a corporation or an S corporation.
- A new LLC with one owner (Single Member LLC) is formed under state law, and has an

excise tax filing requirement for tax periods beginning on or after January 1, 2008 or an employment tax filing requirement for wages paid on or after January 1, 2009.

You **will not be** required to obtain a new EIN if any of the following statements are true.

- You report income tax as a branch or division of a corporation or other entity, and the LLC has no employees or excise tax liability.
- An existing partnership converts to an LLC classified as a partnership.
- The LLC name or location changes.
- An LLC that already has an EIN chooses to be taxed as a corporation or as an S corporation.
- A new LLC with one owner (single member LLC) is formed under state law, does not choose to be taxed as a corporation or S corporation, and has no employees or excise tax liability. **NOTE:** *You may request an EIN for banking or state tax purposes, but an EIN is not required for federal tax purposes.*

Estates

You **will be** required to obtain a new EIN if any of the following statements are true.

- A trust is created with funds from the estate (not simply a continuation of the estate).
- You represent an estate that operates a business after the owner's death.

You **will not** be required to obtain a new EIN if any of the following statement is true.

- The administrator, personal representative, or executor changes his/her name or address.

Trusts

You **will be** required to obtain a new EIN if any of the following statements are true.

- One person is the grantor/maker of many trusts.
- A trust changes to an estate.
- A living or intervivos trust changes to a testamentary trust.
- A living trust terminates by distributing its property to a residual trust.

You **will not** be required to obtain a new EIN if any of the following statements are true.

- The trustee changes.
- The grantor or beneficiary changes his/her name or address.

Sales Tax and Business License

You will also need to obtain a Sales Tax (Reseller's) License, which is obtained through the State Board of Equalization. This is the authority that governs taxes you must charge to customers, if you are doing business over the Internet you are only required to charge sales tax to customers purchasing within the same state you have a business located, however this can change so I recommended you check with the State Board of Equalization on exact tax laws. This is also the authority to which you will be paying the sales tax collected from customers.

> **TIP:** Put any sales tax you collect in a separate bank account so you are not tempted to use it and then get in a bind when it comes time to pay, because the State Board of Equalization does not play around, they can revoke your license, shut your business down, and charge you penalties and/or interest.

You obtain a Business License from the city in which you plan to do business, if it is a home/office then it would be the city in which the home is located. The business license gives you the right to sell products or services within that city. If you sell products to a customer located in another city and ship to them or they ship you reels for service then you only need one business license for the city in which the business is located.

Multiple business licenses usually only are needed if for example you were selling a product and you traveled to different trade shows in multiple cities where you actively sold the product at the show, then you would need a business license for each city. If you are attending a trade show or other function in another city for use of promoting your business, take five minutes and call the State Board of Equalization to find out any requirements you need to meet. It's always better to be safe than sorry.

Sales tax is not applicable to repair service (labor) charges. This could change in the future so keep up with current tax laws; a good accountant will alert you to this change if it ever happens.

Bank Accounts and Credit Cards

When you are checking around for which bank to use for your business banking, there are several things to consider. First, compare rates, check costs, additional fees, separate teller for business accounts, although some banks offer head of line privileges for business account holders, how would you like to walk ahead of 20 other people standing in line and proclaim "I am next", I didn't think so. Secondly, I suggest you use two separate banks and I will explain why.

At the first bank you should open your primary business checking account and a savings account. The checking account will be used for taking customer payment, and cash/check/credit card deposits. The savings account should be used only for transferring your collected sales tax to, this keeps it separated for you.

The second bank, open a secondary business checking, this will be used for transferring money from your primary bank checking account. Once per week or more often if you like, you need to transfer the money from the primary bank checking account to this secondary account. This account you will use for paying debts, creditors, etc. This might sound like a hassle but trust me it can save you great sorrow one day.

The purpose of this is because when you have customers pay by credit card, and for any reason they dispute that charge, and **I mean any reason**, the bank will automatically take that money from your account until the dispute is settled. For a small business man this can cause a lot of problems, especially when the bank does not notify you that it pulled the money. By taking the money out periodically and putting it into another bank there will not be money sitting in that account for them to pull and the bank will be forced to notify you, and they are not allowed to charge any overdraft fee.

I had this happen before in one of my businesses. A customer disputed a charge because he felt he should have been given free lessons on the use of a product he had purchased. Luckily I made all my customers sign receipts and on the receipt I plainly stated that they agreed that purchasing the product did not include teaching them the use of any said product. Although I did try to work with the customer and took time away to try to teach him the basics, but after 4 weeks of daily questions and interruptions, I gave up and firmly told him I could suggest possible paid services from local companies that could give him more time. Of course he called his credit card company and disputed the charge for the product. The bank pulled money from my account without notifying me, I had checks returned that had been sent out to creditors. It took me 4 months, and during this whole time the customer enjoyed the use of the product, to resolve the case and get the money back. But in the meantime I had already spent unnecessary extra money on overdraft fees, returned check fees, not to mention the embarrassment of trying to explain to creditors and vendors.

Credit Cards, what can I say, if you don't take them as a form of payment then you are missing out on about 75% of customers. Let's face it, we live in a plastic world, not just because more rely on plastic to pay for things, but because people feel insured if they have a dispute with a business they have a better chance at retribution against a store owner if they are not satisfied with a service by just simply contacting the credit card company and disputing the charges (Remember, any reason at all).

There are many companies that will provide credit card services, your bank being one of them so you should check with them first. Here are a few things to ask them:

1. What is the percentage of the sale do they get, and different cards have different percentages (MasterCard/Visa, American Express, Discover)
2. Is it extra if you key the credit card number in versus swiping the card in a machine? Since you might do more reels servicing through the mail than in person, it might be a factor for you.
3. Is there a batch fee? Usually when you run credit cards they do not get deposited into your account right away, the funds/credit is just verified and approved, then at the end of the day you run what is called a batch report. This is in effect telling the credit processing company the sales are final and to charge them and deposit the money in your bank account. Credit processing services usually charge you for each batch you run, so only batch once per day at the end of the day if you can help it.

Accountants and CPAs

A good accountant is indispensible to the financial health of your business. As a smart business owner you should be keeping detailed records of sales, payables and receipts all throughout the year so that come tax time when you take everything to the accountant it will be organized and the process will go smoothly and quickly.

Yes, you can bring in a huge unorganized mess with items missing that the accountant needs and you can also pay a huge bill to your accountant because remember most are paid by the hour.

There are several great software packages out there that will take care of handling just about every aspect of your business so you can focus more on your customers. Intuit Quickbooks™ and Peachtree Accounting™ is an example of such software, for the beginner unless you have a lot of financial software experience; I would suggest Intuit Quickbooks™. It is user friendly, will track everything from customer orders, vendor orders, sales, taxes, employees and a whole lot more. The cost if reasonable considering the time and headaches it will save you. However if you want to go the more traditional older route of pen and paper and shoebox, then by all means do it, but make sure you keep it all well organized because you never know when the tax man might want to see it.

The best place to find a good accountant is through word of mouth, that's the way I found mine. If an accountant it really good and is saving a company more money than he is costing them then word will spread among business owners, so ask other local businesses who they use and if they are happy with his or her services.

There is no substitute for knowledge!

"I think that only daring speculation can lead us further and not accumulation of facts." ~ Albert Einstein

What You Need To Get Started

When I first decided to write this book, I of course did a lot of research including ordering and reviewing the only two other books written even closely on the subject of starting a reel repair business, only available in eBook format. I was totally amazed at how outdated, inaccurate, and minimal knowledge these books covered, I felt sad for anyone who wanted to start a new reel repair business and this was all they had to go by.

Which made my quest of writing the best How-To book on starting a reel repair business seem even that much more important. In this book I will be discussing real life experiences that you can put to use in the world today, not some outdated material that might have been relevant 40 years ago, instead I will bring your business into the 21st Century.

Success can be defined in many different ways, depending on what your goals for your business are, whether it is a few repair jobs on the weekends to keep you business, or if you have dreams of having several repair technicians working for you to keep up with demands. If you're one of the former then a marketing plan geared to your local area might suffice, if you are of the latter then you will need to branch out from the local area and the best way you can do that is with the advantage of the Internet.

How To Start A Reel Repair Business | 29

I'm going to assume for the rest of this book that you want your business to takeoff and grow or you would not have purchased this book. If you want to follow the examples in this book that I am going to talk about then <u>you need a good computer to use for your business</u>. If you don't know how to use a computer then you first need to take some classes and learn how to use it, particularly Internet and Mail. Your other alternative is to have a family

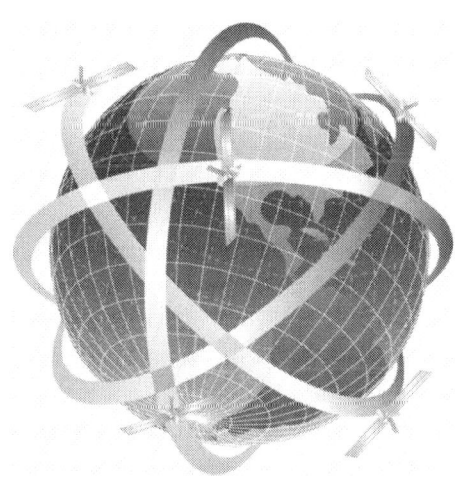

member help you or hire a professional. If you do hire a professional ask for examples of former work, and keep a close eye on costs as it can be quite expensive.

I mentioned earlier there are roughly 82 million anglers in the United States, not all of whom use the Internet but roughly 70% do, and of the remaining other 30%, their friends and family use it. Those are all potential customers that you should be trying to reach; in fact that should be one of your most important goals is to be continually trying every means to reach more customers. Marketing yourself and your services is the key to the success of any business, small or large. Even huge multi-billion dollar businesses never stop marketing their products, the day you do is the day your business turns downhill.

The Internet brought with it a whole new world for businesses, ways of connecting with customers all over the world at the click of a button. If you are only looking to start your business to support local hometown reel repair then you can get by on word of mouth, but for the serious business owner I cannot express enough how important it is that you get plugged in!

There are many ways to use the power of the Internet to your advantage, such as targeted newsletters, mailing lists, sending out specials, etc. We will discuss this in depth in a later section.

You should always be collecting customers email addresses, the same as you would their phone number or mailing address. It is even more so universally accepted these days to give someone your email address than your phone number. Collect customer email address to using for a mailing list for a newsletter, or if you want to run a special price on a service this is a fantastic way to get the word out quickly to all your customers. But don't make the mistake of always trying to sell, sell, sell, or you will drive your emails right into their spam box, instead mix it up with informative materials they will want to read, like a article about maintenance or a new reel model, etc.

Tools and Equipment

Screwdrivers

1/8" Standard
3/16" Standard
5/16" Standard
No.0 Phillips
No.1 Phillips
No.2 Phillips

Others

Standard Sewing Needle
Toothpicks
Cotton Swabs
Lint Free Cloths
Tweezers
6" Calipers
Shimano and Penn Wrenches
Hair Dryer for drying parts

Socket Wrenches

5mm or 3/16"
6mm or 1/14"
7mm or 9/32"
8 mm or 5/16"
9mm or 11/32"
10mm or 13/32"
12mm or 15/32"
14mm or 9/16"

Recommended Lubricants

ReelSchematic Chile Pepper Sauce
ReelSchematic Muscle Grease
ReelSchematic Muscle Lube
ReelSchematic Super Slick

Pliers

Long needle nose
Diagonal Cutting
Snap Ring Pliers

You will also need small containers to hold parts, and cleaning containers.

Pricing Your Services

This is the area where most new reel repair businesses have a problem. When you start pricing your services you should look at your competitors pricing, not just other local repair shops but repair shops across the state and sometimes across the country as well. Prices are market driven, and will change at different times, the key is that your business remain flexible, and adjust for certain things like a lowering economy, however I have found that sometimes instead of lowering the price of a service you can add an additional service that may only take you 10 extra minutes to perform but will help you stand out from your competitors. You can also offer small discounts for multiple reels, or expedited services.

After surveying your competitor's rates, you may be tempted to price your services lower, thinking you'll gain a competitive advantage. This would be a mistake, as prospective clients are more likely to base their buying decisions on "value" than price when choosing between similar services. Decide how you'll add value by offering special features that clients will find worth paying a bit extra to obtain.

Your rates will depend on three things: Your actual costs plus a reasonable profit margin, the pricing the market will bear and the ways you'll add value to your service offering.

Repeat customers are the lifeblood of any business and are also excellent spokespersons for your business, so you should consider giving them a discount for their loyalty. Not only does this let the customer know that you appreciate their business but also will encourage them to tell more people they know about your quality of service. Everyone likes to feel they are treated special and it is human nature to want to tell others, word of mouth is the best form of advertising for your business, friends listen to other friends and other family members more than any traditional advertising.

The unsatisfied customer, not every customer can be satisfied, but it is imperative especially in today's electronic world that you go above and beyond trying to do so. Why? Because there is nothing worse that can damage a business then a disgruntled customer that blasts your business on every website, to every friend, and family member he or she can find. I have myself at times refunded, performed extra work, and even done work for free, even when I had to bite my tongue and it churned my stomach to do it, but remain focused on the big picture and before long your reputation will be of a business that cares about its customers and goes out of its way to ensure they are satisfied. Those same disgruntled customers can become your biggest advertisers for your business, and you will be amazed how loyal they will be to you. Remember, business is not a place for emotional decisions.

Customers are also one of the most valuable resources you have in improving your business; don't be afraid to ask them for comments. Ask them how they feel about the pricing, is it fair to them, what have they paid at other places in the past. People appreciate when you take the time to ask them their opinions and will be happy to share information with you that you can use to fine tune your business approach.

When you are creating your price sheet, make it as simple as possible while still clearly stating what fees are for specific services, for example:

<u>Reel Cleaning</u>
$14.95 per reel
$17.95 per reel for 4/0 and up
$34.95 per Saltwater (lever drag) reel
$37.95 per Saltwater (two-speed lever drag) reel

This lets your customers know clearly what to expect for having services performed. If parts are extra, or you offer specialized grease/oil at an extra cost then you need to state that in your price sheet.

Also be sure to state the services that make you stand out from your competitors, such as expedited service, free exterior cleaning, discounts for repeat customers, etc.

You should also state the brands and types of maintenance products you use such as Grease and Oil, so that the customer knows that you use only the highest quality products in their reels during servicing.

You should include any other pertinent information your customer will appreciate knowing such as the average turnaround time for service, if its 24 hours, or 3 days, tell them. The more you tell them up front, the more they will appreciate it because no one likes surprises, unless it's your birthday.

Employees

At first you might start your business off with only one employee, yourself, which is very common, but eventually as your business grows it may become necessary to hire additional employees. There are good employees and there are bad employees, one can benefit your business and the other can damage it. There are no set in stone rules as to how to pick the right employee but there are things that you can do to narrow your selection.

Have them fill out an employee application, including references, and check ALL the references to get a feel of the kind of employee they might be. Ask things such as, do they get along with others, are they on time, do quality work, etc. Personally I don't know if there is a perfect employee no more than there is any perfect human being. Everyone has good traits and bad traits; it's a mixture of whether the good outweighs the bad that you have to make a decision on.

Hiring employees does not stop there; you will be responsible for paying Workers Compensation, FICA and Medicare for each employee. You should check with your accountant and your insurance provider to determine what those costs will be.

Some first time business owners are able to convince other family members to help them out which can be both good and bad in and of itself, but it will drastically reduce your overhead expenses.

Customer Records

You should also keep organized records of your customers; these records can serve many purposes, from offering discounts to repeat customers, to sending a thank you note.

Again, I recommend Intuit's QuickBooks™ software for this purpose. It is an excellent tool for keeping track of customer information and previous work history. The last thing you want to do to a loyal repeat customer is to keep having to ask for their contact information. Plus you can use this to keep track of what reels your customers own, from this you will start to see a trend for which are most popular and can adjust your parts inventory accordingly.

I also like to track my customers birth dates and send them a 10% off coupon as a gift once a year, you will be surprised just how many will use it every time.

If you can get your customers to give their email addresses this can be a great way to let them know when you are running any specials, and can be used to target repeat customers to give them any special discounts.

Your customers are the lifeline of your business; if you show extra treatment that your competitors do not show then you will win your customers over, and your competitors. You should always make you customer feel like he/she is the most important part of your day, because they are essential to your business's success.

Key Words Customers Love To Hear

"May I"
Ask permission of your customer! Make them feel special!

"As you Know"
These few words used in the beginning of a conversation implies that your customer may already have knowledge about the product or service and that you are just reminding them about those points.

"I'd appreciate it if...."
These words can be used in a conversation to ask the customer to do something that could be helpful such as, "I'd appreciate if the next time you stop in that you could let me know how your daughter liked her jewelry

"Please"
Ask your Mom if you don't know when to use this one!

"It would be my pleasure"
 Your customers listen to MMFS-AM or Make Me Feel Special About Me, so let them know that you want to go out of your way for them in a nice way.

"Thank you!"
Use this one with sincerity and not like a trained parrot.

Vendor Records

With vendors there are several things that you need to track. Build contact information for all your vendors, including parts availability, any discounts, your sales representative, terms and other details you feel help you determine which vendor to order specific parts from. It can take time to find the right vendor that gives a good fit between service and price.

If you have a good account manager at one of your vendors that has helped you in the past it might be wise to remember them come Christmas time with a simple thank you card. You will be surprised how much a simple card can help you throughout the next year!

Remember, being personable not only applies to your customers but to your vendors as well, because your business relies on both.

I've had vendors give me great price breaks, one's that are normally reserved for the big boys, just because I went the extra mile to let my sales representative know that I appreciated his time and efforts.

This is my personal list of companies I have dealt with in the past for reel parts that I feel confident enough about to pass on to you:

The Reel Doctor
Providing services and repairs for reels, rods, trolling motors, and underwater cameras
8732 – 51 Avenue Edmonton, AB T6E 5E8 Canada
Inside Canada – 1.866.431.0146
Outside Canada – 1.780.431.0146
service@reeldr.com
www.reeldr.com

Bucko's Tackle Service
Reel Parts and Service
191 Stafford Road Fall River, MA 02721
1.508.674.7900
mjbucko@mindspring.com
www.buckosparts.com

Anglers Parts Can
Large Supply of Reel Parts
Box 571 Sun Prairie, WI 53590
1.608.225.5501
www.anglerspartscan.com

Designing Your Website

fruitfulBusiness

Your Online Presence

Why does your business need a website? Only if you want to attract customers! Close to 500 million people world-wide have access to the Internet. No matter what your business is you can't ignore 500 million people. Even if you just want to conduct business within your local community, you want to let people in that community know that you are interested in serving them in any way possible. If you don't your competitors will. In today's business world an online presence is a must have and a reel repair business is no exception.

Excerpt from Entrepreneur Magazine ~ Roy Williams

"Websites are perhaps the most overlooked vehicle of advertising for local, owner-operated businesses. Yes, every retailer needs one. Every dentist, lawyer, accountant and minister needs one. Every café, restaurant, coffee shop and nightclub needs one. Every wholesale supply company needs one.

I'm not suggesting that all these businesses need to actually transact business online. I'm only saying that everyone listed in yesterday's Yellow Pages needs to also be available on the internet today--it's where your customers expect to find you.

Think of your site as a relationship deepener, a half step between your advertising and your front door. Do you suppose it's easier to convince customers to visit your web site or to convince them to get in their car, drive to your store, park that car and walk in your door?

The internet is heaven on earth for the 49 percent of our population who are introverted. That's because introverts strongly prefer to gather information anonymously. They're unlikely to dial your phone number, except as a last resort. Even more unlikely is that they'll choose to walk into your store and engage a salesperson. Introverts aren't necessarily shy--they simply like to gather all the facts before they put themselves in a position where they'll likely be asked to answer questions. Forty-nine percent of your customers strongly prefer to know *what* they're coming to buy *before* they walk in your door. And even the extroverted 51 percent of your target market will appreciate an informative site that functions as an expert salesperson during all those hours you're not open for business.

Don't think for a moment that your customers aren't already online. Several times a month, I speak to groups of at least several hundred people. And I always ask, "How many of you have used a search engine within the past seven days to research a product or service that you were considering purchasing?" I raise my own hand as soon as the question is finished. The hands raised in response have never been less than 85 to 90 percent of the crowd."

Your website is one of your most valuable marketing tools you will own. I will focus a lot in this area because the way your website operates, and is built from its foundation will make the difference of whether you are known by thousands of anglers and at the top of search engines lists, or if you are lost among the other billions of sites.

A lot of time and planning must go into your site; top professionals are paid thousands of dollars by corporations to get them the best exposure on search engines they can. You will see this referred to as SEO, Search Engine Optimization, among website owners and developers. I will show you the secrets to doing all this by yourself to get the same results that SEO Experts are paid big bucks to do.

Most are very simple, but attention to detail is the key to success.

Now I am not saying that your online website development, marketing, and maintenance will not cost you anything, because it will, but I will show you ways to reduce the amount of money that you have to spend to get things done right.

Tips when designing your website:

1. Do not use image backgrounds. No single professional, respected site will ever use image backgrounds. It just screams low quality to your potential customers.
2. Don't use overly huge type; it just looks bad for design, too small text can have the same effect. 12 to 13px Arial, or 11 to 12 Verdana works great.
3. Design your color scheme well. Don't use wildly neon colors or colors that do not match together. You wouldn't paint your house neon green so don't paint your website that way either.
4. Don't annoy visitors with pop-up windows, nobody like them!
5. Don't distract your visitors with blinking or scrolling text, animated gif's, or sound.
6. Don't use frames, for one the address bar doesn't change from page to page, making it impossible for a person to bookmark a page.

7. Lines of test should never be more than 600 pixels wide; this makes it easier for the reader after reading one line to find the next. There is a reason newspapers print in columns, it makes it easier for the reader by having short lines.
8. Don't make your pages any wider than 1000 pixels. Most users have a 1024x768 monitor, so pages need to be completely visible at 1000 pixels without horizontal scrolling.
9. Don't use poor text colors on poor background colors, as if this tip isn't obvious enough, then why did I run across this site today?

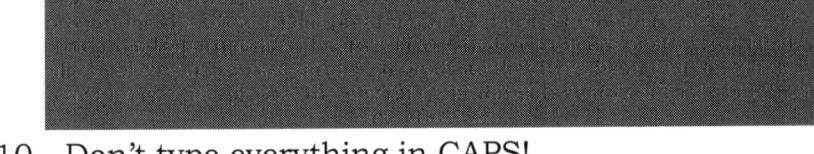

10. Don't type everything in CAPS!
11. Never use more than one exclamation point! Using multiple exclamation points does not make your text seem any more important that just one and it screams "Amateurish!" or "Desperate!" Do exclamation marks really impress you when you read them? Are you more likely to believe something because it has a screaming mark at the end? It's probably the opposite: You're used to desperate marketers trying to sell you something with their exclamation marks, so when you see lots of them you sense that

desperation and tend to discount what they're trying to convince you of.
12. Do not underline words that are not links. On the web underlined words are suppose to be links.
13. Don't ask to exchange links with other sites. I know this goes against a lot of popular belief. Link exchange requests are only a little less annoying than "permission to link" requests and completely useless. Link to other sites if you think they'll be of value or interest to your readers -- not because the other site links back. If you want links to your site, make your site *worthy* of being linked to, link to other worthy sites, and then ask those other sites for a *link* (not a link *exchange*). Don't make your link to them contingent on whether they link back or not. If they're worth linking to, they're still worth linking to even if they don't link back.

If you would like some more examples of what not to do, here is a great site to visit to see what is out there: http://www.problemwebsites.com

Domain Names and Website Hosting

Ok, let's start with your domain name. When you were selecting your business name you should have already checked that the name is also available as a domain name, i.e. "The Reel Doctor" and www.thereeldoctor.com There are several domain suffixes available like .com, .biz, .tv, .org, but your primary site should use .com because this is the most universally recognized suffix and will be the one that customers remember the easiest.

There is a galore of places that you can go to online to register your domain name, and all do the same thing, register the domain name with ICANN. There are many companies that are not accredited by ICANN offer domain registration services, some are reselling names obtained from other accredited registrars, talk about middle men. If you want to know if the company you are using is an accredited registrar and not just a middle man check here http://www.internic.net/problem_reports/p10.html.

Prices may vary from place to place so you should look around. Always be aware of the up-sell products that they will tell you that you need, for example making your register information private, registrars took this same scam from the phone companies by telling you to pay to not have your information listed publicly. You can register for several different years, i.e. 1, 2,3,4,5 years at a time, the cost usually being lower the more years that you register for upfront, and being your business you might want to register for the most length of time that you can afford because it can be easy to forget in 1 or 2 years to renew it, and yes if you do not renew it someone else could purchase it out from under you. Most registrars does offer auto-new which will at least remind you it is time for renewal.

Same goes for a company to host your website; this is the company that will host the website pages on a server for access by Internet users. There are many different hosting companies with different services, far too many for me to list here, so it pays to shop around for the best deal but also with the best service.

One company I have used in the past and have been very satisfied with is a company called Hostgator, www.hostgator.com, I have been pleased with their services and quick response times and resolution anytime I did have an issue 24/7/365.

Your Business's Email

Every hosting company is going to give you email with your website hosting account in the form of your domain name, such as @reelmechanic.com. It is an absolute must that you use your business email address with every piece of correspondence that you send out or reply to, don't be using your free Yahoo, Gmail, or AOL account for your business. Nothing looks more unprofessional than to get an email from a business that's from bob@yahoo.com. You want your company to have a professional appeal, so use an email address that sounds professional. Can you imagine if Daiwa used yahoo as their mail, how confident would customers have felt dealing with a company that doesn't use its own company email?

Besides this is all part of "branding" on your business name, you should by now be eating, sleeping and thinking your business name. You should be using your business name in everything that you do, answering the phone, sending emails, letterhead, invoices, etc. Why do you think the popular brands are so recognized, because they use their business logo and name in every single thing they do. It's called Brand Recognition!

In a later chapter I will discuss the importance of email marketing and how it can make your business boom!

Remember to answer all emails promptly, an unanswered email could mean a lost customer!

Solid Foundation

There are basic foundations to your website development that you need to know whether you are building the site yourself or having a professional build it. If you are inexperienced in website design then I highly suggest you seek the services of a professional to help you build it. I'm not talking about the cookie cutter designers that offer to build your site for $19.95.

There are places sites that can help you find great developers at a discount price, one of which is www.elance.com, you will need to post your design requirements and then you will start getting bids from all over the world. If you're lucky and no how to do web design then you can save yourself a lot of money, but do expect if you want it to be good you will need to dedicate many, many hours. If you are unsure but think you can do it, then trust me, hire a professional.

TIP: If your brother-in-law, sister or any other family member says they can do It because they've been the family computer guy, don't go that route unless they can give you examples of previous work they have done, treat it just like you would as if you were hiring a stranger.

I can't count the number of times I've heard the story how someone has a brother-in-law, sister, or some family member that is supposed to be a web design guru, and they can build the site. But for some reason it just isn't getting the traffic or rankings they hoped for. It's usually because it was not built correctly from the foundation up. So use a professional if you want your business to grow outside your local community, where people tend to be more forgiving because they know you, the outside world – not so forgiving.

Meta Tags

ALL META TAGS RESIDE BETWEEN THE <HEAD> AND </HEAD> TAGS IN THE HTML OF EACH PAGE.

Meta elements provide information about a given webpage, most often to help search engines categorize them correctly. Though not the main factor search engines consider when ranking site, you still should not leave them off a page. Over the years webmasters have abused these tags to be deceptive that search engines have had to de-emphasize their importance in their algorithms. They are inserted into the HTML document, but are often not directly visible to a user visiting the site. There are several META Tags, below are listed the three most important that you need to be familiar with:

TITLE
<meta name="title" content="The Reel Mechanic" />

DESCRIPTION
<meta name="description" content="The Reel Mechanic specializes in repairing fishing reels from all major reel manufacturers." />

KEYWORD
<meta name="keywords" content="fishing reels, fishing, reel maintenance, reel cleaning" />

"Keywords"

You should come up with a list of at least 10 key words that are most relevant for the search engine to index the page. When you are coming up with keywords, think about what words or phrases your customers might type in a search engine to find you. These should be as unique as you can make them but it is an absolute must they accurately pertain to your business. The maximum amount of keywords or phrases should be between 500-700 characters. Such as "Reel Repairs", "Reel Maintenance", "Reel Upgrades", don't use more than two words in each keyword, keep it simple and short. These must also be words that you will use on your website pages, but not so many times that search engines think you are trying to trick them and penalize your site, 5-6 times on a page is about right and the higher on the beginning of the page the better.

Search engines feel that if a keyword is relevant to your site then you will be using that word(s) often on your site pages, and it should be in the beginning of the page since it would be important to your business. Many businesses spend an extensive amount of time and money doing in-depth analysis on keywords, if you think logically, keywords are really words that a person might type into a search engine page if they were looking for a site that pertained to a particular subject. For example if I was looking to have my reel repaired, I might type "reel repair" in the search engine. This is what your goal is, to get yourself to come up in the 1st or 2nd listing on the first page of any search engine results. In reality there is much more that goes into getting ranking in the top 1 to 5 spots on a search engine than just keywords and we will touch on that as well.

Keywords are listed in the following html format:
<meta name="keywords" content="reel repair, reel maintenance, reel upgrades " />

"Title"

This is what search engines use for indexing the name of your page. This should be different for every page of your website, and should be relevant to the content on the page.

<meta name="title" content="The Fishing Reel Mechanic" />

Or for another page

<meta name="title" content="The Fishing Reel Mechanic Maintenance Services" />

"Description"

This is where you place a description of the page, and it should be different for every page. Remember this is included in the listing you will see in a search engine results so it should be very informative and relevant to content for that particular page.

```
<meta name="description" content="The Fishing Reel Mechanic
specializes in repairing fishing reels from all major reel
manufacturers." />
```

Image Tags and Link Titles

This is an area that most people over look. Every image on a webpage has an image tag which is used to describe the image. It was long used extensively in the past when slower internet connections were a big concern and people turned off image displaying in their browser to speed up webpage loading, the description was instead shown. Fortunately, today with almost every home having a high-speed Internet connection it is rare that anyone turns off image displaying. However search engine still index these descriptions, so you should be taking advantage of that by putting descriptive content in them to provide an even more robust page for search engine indexing.

```
<img src="/repair/peenreel.jpg" alt="Penn Reel">
```

Each link that you place on your site can include a link title, and this is widely used for giving the visitor a description of the link when they hover their mouse over the link. I've been using them for the several years, and have very good results. My results may be because of everything else I do, but either way it's not hurting rankings either and it won't hurt yours.

`<a href="/repair/" title="Reel Repair Pricing">Reel Repair Pricing</a>`

TOP SEARCH ENGINE OPTIMIZATION TIPS (SEO)

a. **Be Bold**. Use the `<b>` `</b>` tags around specific keywords that deal with your business but in keeping with not overdoing it and risk making your site look unappealing.

b. **Inbound Links.** You need to gain links from other sites, this weighs heavily with search engines because it tell the search engines that you must have content worthwhile. You can do this by publishing informative articles on your site and letting other know they are there, that will lead people to post links to the article in other forums, blogs, etc. You want these incoming links going to all pages of your site, if inbound links only point to your home page then it makes the site look shallow to search engines, so spread good content around different pages on your site.

TIP: Stay away from link exchange directories and link pages, these do no good and some search engines will actually penalize you for being on them. Good links are built from good content, nothing else; there is no magic and no overnight solution.

c. **Newsletters.** This can be a great way to publish regular news and content to your customers, and let you collect contact information about your customers. A great monthly newsletter can go a long way; it helps to remind the customer to come back to your site, what specials you may have running, and keeps you in the back of their mind when they need reel service. Remember to remain complaint with current CAN-SPAM Act you need to give your customers the ability to opt-out of emailing. Read more about the legalities of using email:

http://www.ftc.gov/bcp/edu/pubs/business/ecommerce/bus61.shtm

d. **No Broken Links.** This seems simple and it is but many people do not check the links in their site regularly. If you link to outside resources or sites, they can change pages without your notice so you should check your links on a regular basis. Make sure all your links are always correct and unbroken. Search engines that come across these broken links, whether or not they penalize you for it or not does not benefit you because the search engine cannot follow the link.

Reel Maintenance

Modern reels are complex pieces of equipment; super smooth, multiple bearings, high-tech lightweight materials, you name it. Unfortunately this high-tech gear comes at a price.

Even though most tackle is made from high quality materials like carbon, aviation grade aluminum, stainless steel and even titanium, we practice our sport in a very hostile environment: humidity, UV exposure, extreme temperatures, salt spray, mud, sand, coral....

In spite of the quality of design and material, fishing reels take a beating every time we go out. Does this mean that you should only buy less expensive equipment? Certainly not, however there are some things that you can do to properly care for and maintain your reels, and this book is going to show you how to do that. Saltwater reels should be rinsed with warm freshwater to remove any saltwater residue, dried, and then lubricated appropriately according to the manufacturer. Saltwater corrodes metal parts quickly; a saltwater reel left unmaintained will quickly corrode and cease to function at all.

Tips for protecting reels:

1. Always avoid dipping your reel in water especially saltwater.

2. Avoid hitting your reel against rocks, docks, boat decks, etc. Scratches and dents can expose bare metal and cause corrosion.

3. Never drop a reel in the sand, sand grains can damage drag disks and ball bearings. If you do, stop using it immediately until you service it!

4. Make sure reels are not exposed to saltwater spray on a moving boat. This is where reel covers should always be used.

5. Immediately after each fishing trip, rinse the reel under LOW pressure freshwater, then remove the spool, shake out any excess water and allow to dry before reassembly. Reels should never be soaked for extended periods of time because water will penetrate ball bearings and cause them to rust, even though a ball bearing case might be stainless steel, the bearing itself may not be. Soaking can also distort cork drag plates and cause jerky drags.

6. Always loosen the drag completely whenever the reel is not in use. This will prevent damage to the drag washers due to compression.

7. When storing saltwater reels you should remove all line and backing because the line will hold saltwater residue and can cause corrosion.

8. It is better to not store a reel in a pouch or cover, especially if the reel is wet. It is always better to store the reel on a shelf or inside a cabinet.

9. **Fresh water fishing,** if you fish only a few times per year, have your reel serviced at least once every year, two on the outside. If you fish regularly, have your reel serviced once per year minimum.

10. **For salt water fishing,** if you fish only a few times per year, have your reel serviced a minimum of once per year. If you fish on a regular basis your reel should be serviced two to four times per year. You can determine how often by having it serviced at a two to four month interval then ask the servicer how often he recommends by what it looks like internally. This way you could add or reduce service intervals accordingly while getting the maximum life out of your equipment.

11. **For seasonal fishing** it would be wise to have your reel serviced at the end of the fishing season rather than at the beginning of the next season. If moisture were to get inside your reel, then you put it aside for four or five months, some reel parts may become damaged from corrosion. If you're going to have it serviced anyway, the best time is at the end of the fishing season.

Basic Cleaning Tips

1. Gather the proper cleaning supplies.

    1. We recommend you use Simple Green for a general purpose cleaning compound, Lighter Fluid for bearings, ReelSchematic Chile Pepper Sauce Reel Oil, and ReelSchematic Muscle Grease.

2. Never put metal to metal when working on your reel, all parts are designed to be metal to fiber.

3. Never use gasoline or other petroleum based products to remove dirt and grease from reel parts, it can and will melt plastic parts. Instead use a cleaning product such as Simple Green which will not hurt plastic and fiber parts.

4. When you are greasing gears, always apply the grease to the bottoms of the teeth, this will avoid grease splatter. Remember a light coat is all you need so don't apply to much.

5. Clean bearings with lighter fluid to remove dirt and buildup. After you've got them all clean make sure they spin, if they don't then you know they are not clean enough yet. When you get them cleaned oil them with ReelSchematic Chile Pepper Sauce Oil, you should only need one drop for each bearing.

Lubrication

The main purpose of any lubricant in a reel is to reduce wear. Generally grease will be used on bushings, gear teeth, and shafts to prevent metal to metal contact. The most essential property of grease is its viscosity, you'll hear this term a lot when referring to both grease and oil. **Viscosity** is a measure of the resistance of a fluid which is being deformed by either shear stress or extensional stress. In everyday terms (and for fluids only), viscosity is "thickness". Thus, water is "thin", having a lower viscosity, while honey is "thick" having a higher viscosity. The viscosity of the grease you are using must be sufficient to resist extrusion from the contacting metal surfaces by the pressure generated by heavy loads, and it must be unaffected by temperature and water.

The latest in nano-technological advances is Tungsten Disulfide (WS_2). The most lubricious material known to modern science is now being combined with high quality synthetic lubricants to produce a grease that is unmatched by others. Tungsten Disulfide can be used in high temperatures and high pressure application. It offers temperature resistance from -4° F to 1472° F, and a load bearing weight of 300,000 psi.

"Super Slick" is specifically formulated with

Tungsten Disulfide to provide the best grease known to science for fishing reels.

Tungsten Disulfide (WS2) is one of the most lubricious materials known to science. With Coefficient of Friction at 0.03, it offers excellent dry lubricity unmatched to any other substance. It can also be used in high temperature and high pressure applications. It offers temperature resistance from -450° F (-270° C) to 1200° F (650° C) in normal atmosphere and from -305° F (-188° C) to 2400° F (1316° C) in Vacuum. Load bearing property of coated film is extremely high at 300,000 psi.

Tungsten Disulfide (WS2) can be used instead of Molybdenum Disulfide (MoS2) and Graphite in almost all applications, and even more. Molybdenum and Tungsten are from same chemical family. Tungsten is heavier and more stable. Molybdenum Disulfide (Also known as Moly Disulfide) till now has been extremely popular due to cheaper price, easier availability and strong and innovative marketing. Tungsten Disulfide is not new chemical and has been around as long as Moly, and is used extensively by NASA, military, aerospace and automotive industry.

Till few years ago, price was Tungsten Disulfide was almost 10 times that of Molybdenum Disulfide. But since then price of Molybdenum Disulfide has doubled every six months. Now the prices of both chemicals are within comparable range. Now, it makes more economic sense to use superior dry lubricant (Tungsten Disulfide) and improve the quality and competitiveness of final product.

Tungsten Disulfide offers excellent lubrication under extreme conditions of Load, Vacuum and Temperature. The properties below show that Tungsten Disulfide offers excellent thermal stability and oxidation resistance at higher temperatures. WS2 has thermal stability advantage of 93°C (200°F) over MoS2. Coefficient of Friction of WS2 actually reduces at higher loads.

"Super Slick" is a technological breakthrough in nano-lubricants. Super Slick has the lowest coefficient of friction of any grease in the world; it offers lubricity unmatched by any other substance! If you're looking for the absolute best lubricating grease in the world for your reels this is it! **Tungsten Disulfide**, which is known to be the most lubricious material known to science, was once only used extensively by NASA, Aerospace, and Military because of its price. Today it is available to you in our newest "Super Slick" Grease.

- The lowest coefficient of friction of any substance in the world - .015
- Temperature resistance from -4 F (-20 C) to 1472 F (800 C)
- It will hold up in even the worst of weather conditions!
- Excellent extreme pressure properties with loading bearing up to 300,000 psi
- Extremely high resistance to water, rust and humidity
- High dropping point of 608° F which means it does not solidify at high temperatures
- 100x better than any grease you are presently using!

Available at www.reelschematic.com

Typical Bait Casting Reel Lubrication

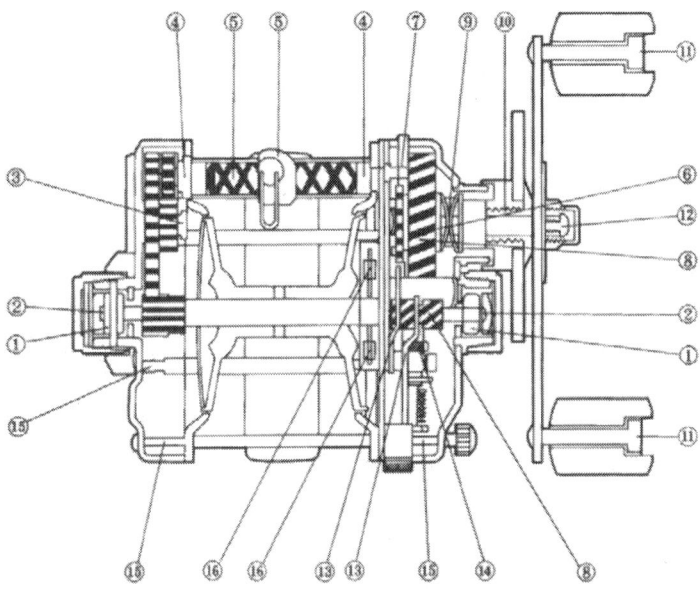

© Photo courtesy of Daiwa Corporation

How To Start A Reel Repair Business | 65

#	Part Name	Lubrication	How Often	Key Point Care
1	Ball Bearing	Medium or heavy oil Light or medium grease	After each day of fishing Once every 3 weeks	Do not drop or hit. Always keep bearing greased inside and out
2	Spool Shaft	Medium or heavy oil Light or medium grease	After each day of fishing Once every 3 weeks	Contact or meshing areas of ball bearing or pinion gear
3	Cog wheel & cog wheel holder shaft	Light or medium oil Heavy Oil	Once every 3 weeks Once every 2 months	Do not use heavy grease
4	Worm shaft on shield bushing left & right side	Light or medium oil	After each day of fishing	—
5	Worm shaft & line guide pin	Medium or heavy oil Light or medium grease	Once every 3 weeks Once every 2 months	Regularly inspect for dirt, grit, and salt – keep clean
6	Spool drag washer	Medium or heavy grease	Once every 3 months	Contains special Teflon or graphite grease for better performance
7	A/R claw and gear shaft click	Medium or heavy grease sparingly all areas.	Once every 3 months	Do not disturb the claw spring arrangement
8	Drive gear & pinion gear	Medium or heavy grease	Once every 3 months	Make sure all surfaces are lubricated in appropriate amounts
9	Drag spring & gear shaft assembly	Medium or heavy grease	Once every 3 months	Make sure all surfaces are lubricated

Reel Maintenance

10	Star drag	Medium or heavy grease	Once every 3 months	After each day of fishing, loosen drag adjustment to preserve the spring and washer life
11	Handle knob or shaft	Light or medium heavy oil Light or medium grease	After each day fishing Once every 3 weeks	Inspect regularly. Do not allow lube to dry to eliminate wear
12	Set plate on gear shaft	Medium or heavy oil	Once every 3 weeks	Be certain to remove nut plate screw & plate. Take off nut & screw
13	Clutch lever & set plate post	Medium or heavy grease	Once every 3 months	Lubricate in appropriate amounts
14	Set plate spring A B Pinion yoke spring	Medium or heavy oil	Once every 3 months	Lubricate in appropriate amounts
15	Frame assembly post	Medium or heavy grease	Once every 2 months	Lubricate in appropriate amounts
16	Spool brake collar shaft	Do Not Lubricate	Once every 3 months	No lubrication
17	Spool line	Do Not Lubricate		If saltwater fishing, spool should be removed after each trip and rinsed with freshwater

Typical Spinning Reel Lubrication

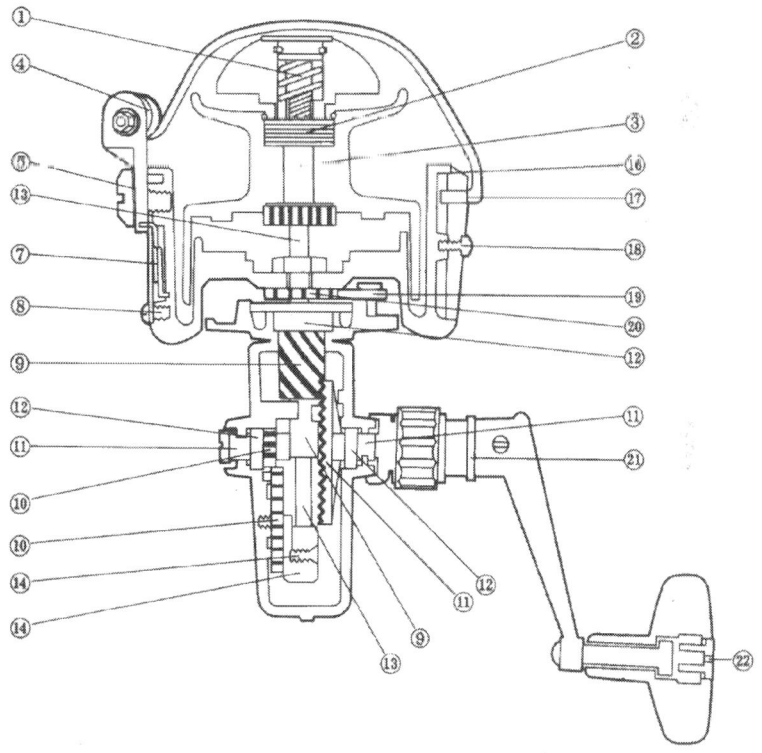

© Photo courtesy of Daiwa Corporation

Reel Maintenance

#	Part Name	Lubrication	How Often	Key Point Care
1	Drag Knob	Medium or heavy grease	Once every 3 weeks	Do not over lubricate, and do not change the sequence of washers
2	Spool Washer	Medium or heavy grease	Once every 3 weeks	Contains special Teflon or graphite grease for better performance
3	Main shaft	Light or medium heavy grease	After each fishing day	Make certain the spool washer is present
4	Line Roller	Light or heavy oil Light or medium grease	After each day fishing Once every 3 weeks	Lubricate in appropriate amounts
5	Arm Lever & Screw	Medium or heavy oil Light or medium heavy grease	After each day fishing Once every 4 weeks	Lubricate in appropriate amounts
6	Arm Lever Screw	Medium or heavy grease	Once every 3 months	Lubricate in appropriate amounts
7	Bail Spring	Medium or heavy grease	Once every 3 months	
8	Bail Spring Cover Screw	Medium or heavy grease	Once every 3 months	
9	Pinion Gear	Light or medium grease	Once every 3 months	Lubricate all surfaces with an appropriate amount
10	Osc. Gear, Osc. Pinion	Medium grease	Once every 3 months	Lubricate all surfaces with an appropriate amount

How To Start A Reel Repair Business | 69

#	Part Name	Lubrication	How Often	Key Point Care
11	Drive Gear	Medium or heavy grease	Once every 3 months	Gear teeth & shaft. Lubricate with appropriate amounts
12	Ball Bearing	Heavy Oil or light grease Medium or heavy grease	Once every 3 months	Freshwater reel only Saltwater reel, all surfaces
13	Main Shaft	Medium or heavy oil Light or medium grease	Once every 3 months 6. 7.	Freshwater Saltwater all surfaces
14	Oscillating Slider	Medium grease	Once every 3 months	Lubricate in appropriate amounts
15	Osc. Slider Screw	Medium grease	Once every 3 months	
16	Rotor assembly	Medium or heavy grease	Once every 3 months	Left & Right Side
17	Bail Assembly	Medium or heavy oil Medium or heavy grease	After each day fishing Once every 3 weeks	
18	Bail Holder Screw	Medium grease	Once every 3 months	
19	A/R Claw & Screw	Heavy Oil Medium or light grease	Once every 3 months	Do not alter claw spring arrangement

Reel Maintenance

20	Ratchet & Screw	Light or medium grease	Once every 3 months	
21	Handle Washer & Screw	Medium oil or grease	Once every 3 weeks	
22	Handle Knob & Shaft	1. Medium or heavy oil 2. Light or medium heavy grease	1. After each day fishing 2. Once every 3 weeks	

REEL REPAIR PICKUP LOCATIONS

This is ideal for local area service if you do your business out of your home. Talk to some store owners at tackle stores, marinas, etc. that do not currently off reel repair services to their customers, and offer to give them 15-20% or flat rate of the profits for every reel that they take into their store for you. This will help defer the costs for their extra time, and also to cover any credit card processing fees if you want them to take credit card payments for you as well as cash.

You can do pickups and drop-offs at these locations twice a week. This gives anglers a convenient place to drop off their reels for repair and in return you get more customers. Remember to leave business cards and service order forms for the customers to fill out, the store owner will collect the reel and then return it to their customer when it is completed, along with collecting the payment due. The more places you can get to do this for you the better.

Pay the store owner their percentage right away when you do your rounds, and always make sure to ask the owner if there are any issues that you need to address. The easier you make it for the store owner, the more receptive he or she will be to working with you.

Some store owners will be reluctant because they may fear that if you provide a poor service then it will be a direct reflection on their business to their customers. So it is up to you to convince the store owner that you can provide a quality, reliable service to his or her customers that will benefit their business by enabling them to offer an additional service to their customers. If you are awaiting parts, backlogged, etc. it is imperative that you keep both the customer and the store owner informed to avoid any miscommunication.

For more detailed information on Reel Care and Maintenance I recommend my other book "Fishing Reel Care and Maintenance 101", an in depth guide to reel repair.

Available at www.reelschematic.com

Marketing and Advertising

"BEWARE: <u>do not</u> start advertising until your site is 100% complete and you've checked it thoroughly for errors!"

Conventional Advertising

Advertising is one of the most important if not "the most" important part of any new business. This is a good example of poor advertising, how many businesses are just in your local area that you don't even know exist?

There are several ways of doing effective advertising that we will discuss:

a. Contact local stores that compliment the service that you are offering, for example shops that sell reels but don't service them, tackle stores, marinas, bait shops, etc. Ask if you can drop by some information on your new business and if you have some flyers you can ask if you can leave them in their store, in return you might offer to refer your customers to them that might be in the market for purchasing a new reel or tackle.

b. Get listed in your local phone company's yellow pages. Yes, some people do still use it even though the Internet is more prevalent. I wouldn't worry about going for the largest ad, I would instead I will show you later where to put that money to better use in your online advertising campaign.

c. Business cards are essential; you should always have some in your pocket everywhere you go. Advertising for your business is not just a 9 to 5 job, it is a 24/7 job. Hand them

out all the time; tell people who you are, and what services you offer.
d. If you want to go with an ad in a nationally syndicated magazine and you have the budget, then go for it. The more you put your business in the public eye the better.
e. Window decals, for a small price you can get lettering created for your vehicle's back window that lists your business name, phone and website (your logo is also recommended because if make you look more professional). Make sure you get it professionally installed; there is nothing worse than advertising bad work to potential customers.

Email Marketing

This is a great study that was conducted by E-consultancy.com; I highly suggest you give a lot of regard.

E-consultancy and Adestra have published research that reveals that e-mail is a crucial and proven weapon for organizations that are trying to focus on effective marketing during the recession.

The E-mail Census 2009 found that 78 per cent of company respondents now rate e-mail as 'excellent' or 'good' for return on investment (ROI), higher than for any other digital marketing channel and up 12 per cent from 2008.

However, the research also found that significant numbers of marketers are still failing to adopt a range of best practices relating to e-mail, and many are still failing to get to grips with deliverability.

18 per cent of companies know what percentage of their e-mail budget is lost through non-delivery.

The research has also found that lack of e-mail strategy is now more likely to be regarded by company respondents as a significant barrier to effective e-mail marketing, up from 32 per cent of e-mail marketers in 2008 to 44 per cent in 2009.

69 per cent of agency respondents say this is a major barrier for their clients, up 16 per cent since last year.

Linus Gregoriadis, research director at E-consultancy, said: 'While some companies are mastering various tactical elements of e-mail best practice, such as segmentation, deliverability, list cleansing and triggered e-mails, it is clear that there are still problems for many organizations at a strategic level.

'A well thought-out e-mail strategy has to be the starting point for e-mail marketing success.' He added: 'The research shows that e-mail is a crucial weapon for marketers during the recession because, when used properly, it delivers excellent ROI and compares very favorably to other digital marketing channels.' The research found that, on average, 42 per cent of e-mails (by volume) sent by responding organizations are acquisition-focused compared to 58 per cent for retention-based e-mails.

Additionally, there has been a nine per cent increase in the proportion now re-marketing through e-mail as companies attempt to get as much value as possible from existing customers.

But worryingly, the research also found that 42 per cent of e-mail marketers do not know their ROI from e-mail marketing.

Henry Hyder-Smith, managing director at Adestra, said: 'With belts tightening throughout this recession, it is very concerning that 42 per cent of marketers do not know their ROI from e-mail marketing.

'It is the most cost-effective medium, accounting for just 14 per cent of online marketing budgets.

'With many marketers recording ROIs of more than six times, budget constraints should not be seen as a barrier.' The E-mail Census also revealed that application service providers/hosted service is now the most commonly adopted method for e-mail marketing, with nearly half of company e-mail marketers (47 per cent) using this approach.

The use of a web-based application interface has increased massively in the last two years, up from 27 per cent of respondents 2007.

75 per cent of respondents are now carrying out basic segmentation, with a further 19 per cent of company e-mail marketers planning to implement this.

The next most commonly undertaken e-mail marketing practice is regular list cleansing, currently undertaken by 60 per cent of companies.

The vast majority of e-mail marketers (72 per cent) say that they are not using e-mail marketing as effectively as they could.

Only 16 per cent are using e-mail as effectively as possible for acquisition compared to 24 per cent for retention.

Google™ Adwords™

If you've used the Internet even remotely then you definitely know who "Google"™ is, they are the world's most popular search engine used my millions of Internet users each day. You've probably also seen their adwords on websites, their search engine results, Gmail, and other places.

To access Google™ Adwords go here http://adwords.google.com

Some of the benefits are:

- **Expand your marketing presence.** With AdWords, you can get the attention of people entering over two hundred million search queries per day.
- **Get qualified leads.** Your ads appear when people search for keywords you choose for your business. You're reaching an audience already interested in what you have to offer.
- **Earn more.** With AdSense, you make money when people click your site's Google ads. Imagine the additional revenue you can earn through AdWords.

- **Keep your costs down.** Relevant AdWords ads get better placement. If your ads are targeted, you can enjoy the most visible positions without necessarily paying more.
- **Focus on your business outside of advertising.** Create your ads. Set your budget. Activate your account. Then let AdWords bring new customers to you.

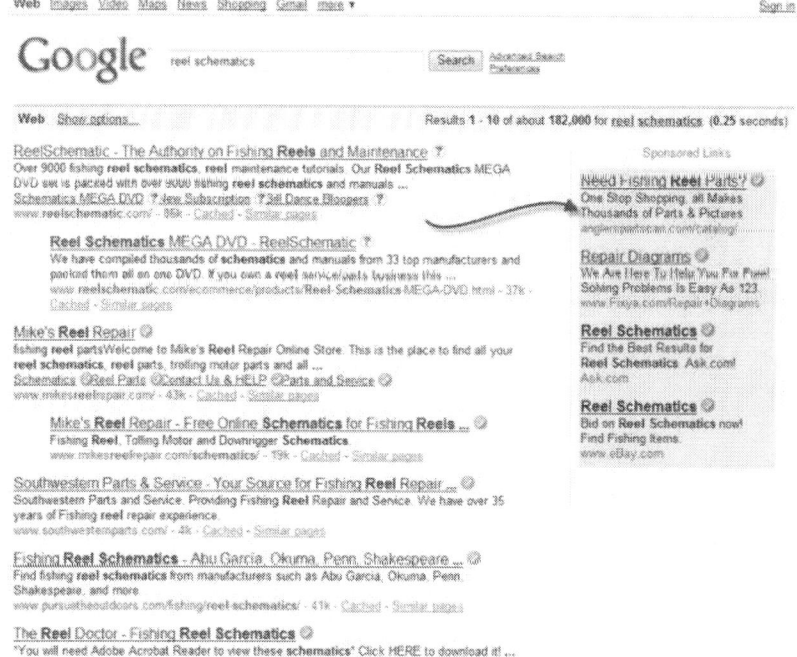

In the above example of a Google™ search results page, you can see the adword results listed on the right.

You set the budget that you are willing to spend each month, and Google™ will automatically adjust the amount that your ad is displayed based on a very complex algorithm. Each time someone clicks on your ad it costs you a small amount of money, just how much depends on the keyword that was used when your ad appeared.

Set your budget
There's no minimum spending requirement – the amount you pay for AdWords is up to you. You can, for instance, set a daily budget of five dollars and a maximum cost of ten cents for each click on your Ad.

Avoid guesswork
We provide keyword traffic and cost estimates so you can make informed decisions about choosing keywords and maximizing your budget.

Pay only for results
You're charged only if someone clicks your ad, not when your ad is displayed.

Estimate the cost of keywords
https://adwords.google.com/select/KeywordToolExternal?defaultView=3

Local and regional targeting
Set your ads to appear only to people searching in a particular state, city, or region. Now it's easy to target online customers within, say, 25 miles of your front door.

Local business ads
Get noticed on Google Maps. People searching for information related to your business will see your location, contact information, and an image of your choosing highlighted on a map of your area.

Expand your reach through the content network
With hundreds of thousands of high-quality websites, news pages, and blogs that partner with Google to display AdWords ads, the Google content network can reach users all over the web to help you drive conversions. Choose from text, image, and video formats to communicate your message.

Target the right user in the right context
Using your keywords, Google's contextual targeting technology can automatically match your ads to WebPages in our content network that are most relevant to your business. For example, an ad for a digital camera may show up next to an article reviewing the latest

digital cameras. If you want greater control, use placement targeting to hand-pick specific sites or sections of sites you want your ads to appear on.

Measure and optimize your results
With the Placement Performance Report, you have visibility into where all your ads appear. Review your ad's performance on a site-by-site basis to see impression, click, cost, and conversion data, and use this data to identify well-performing sites to target more aggressively and low-value placements that require content optimization or exclusion.

Advertising on other sites

This can generate some highly targeted traffic to your business. Specifically because you should be advertising on sites that compliment your business, such as tackle stores, marinas, etc. People visiting those sites are definitely your potential customers because they are almost 100% anglers, and every angler owns at least one reel however it is very unusual to see an angler without at least two or three reels in their arsenal.

When I was starting out advertising ReelSchematic, I did some research to find the most trafficked website in each region of the United States, East, Central, Mid-West and West. Those are the sites I choose to run text ads on. Some websites charge more, some less for advertising, and some sites made charge per 1,000 impressions while other charge only a month fee with unlimited impressions.

My experience with local sites has been a text ad will run you about $50-75 per month with unlimited impressions. However, my ad was being viewed an average of 80,000+ times on each site! That's a lot of exposure. Your **click thru rate** (how many times a person actually clicks your ad to go to your site) will run a lot lower, typically about 10% of the **impressions** (how many times the ad is shown to people). But even still, that is about 8,000 people a day!

Click **T**hru **R**atio determines the effectiveness of an ad in terms of click-thrus. It is a ratio of the number of times the ad was clicked on by the viewer and the number of times the ad was displayed. Thus, if an ad has been displayed 1000 times and has been clicked 50 times, its CTR is 50:1000 or 1:20. Changing this CTR into a percentage value yields 5% (1/20 * 100); thus, 5% of the impressions have lead to clicks on the ad.

As part of my research for this book I ran advertising for ReelSchematic on many different sport fishing sites to determine what would give you the best bang for your buck, the best services, and best overall customer service. The extensive review revealed that there were only two major sites that passed all tests for affordability, best advertising services, and best customer service!

East Coast – www.noreast.com
West Coast – www.allcoast.com

If you are interested in reaching the greatest amount of anglers in the least amount of time, you need to be advertising your business on these two sites at least. I tried a lot of sport fishing sites and of all them you will get the most viewers for your money on these two sites.

Both are highly trafficked sites by anglers, text ads will run you $50 a month for each site, with unlimited impressions, and they offer a whole toolbox full of other advertising avenues with them such as advertising in the forums under the "Premium Sponsor Announcements". That section allows a sponsor to make an announcement and be as advertorial as you like in the section. It is true that the section gets less views than other forums but the 50-100 views an announcement gets are valuable ones because they are views by people who are fully aware that the section they are about to read is an ad and yet they still open up and read it.

There are 50,000 registered users of Noreast.com and 49,000 of those registered users willingly accept e-mail advertisements from Nor'east. When they are promoting Nor'east events they send that list an e-mail blast. The blasts get an awesome response. Nor'east looks for many ways to support you even beyond what you pay for; they add value to your advertising by incorporating your business into other venues. For example, they included my business into one of their email newsletters. That went out to the 50,000 plus members registered on noreast.com alone. That promotion itself is a $3,000 value, but they offered it to me as a thank you for advertising with them.

They will monitor the performance of the ad and will send you an update. It is definitely worth considering as part of your advertising arsenal.

Allcoast.com contact:

John C. Baier
Account Manager
Allcoast Media
631-863-0170 xt 27
jbnoreast@gmail.com

Noreast.com contact:

Rob Pavlick
Allcoast Media
631 863 0170 ext. 28
rob.pavlick@gmail.com

Competitors

How To Handle Competitors

It is assured that from time to time this will come up, if not from a competitor themselves than from a customer that tries to compare your services and pricing to another business. The first rule in business is "Never" bad mouth or talk down your competition; this only makes you look unprofessional. Explain to the customer the differences between your services and theirs, and the extra service and care that you can provide them that your competition is not. Your object is not to try to get the customer on your side by talking negative about your competitors but by talking positive about your business and services.

Just because a competitor reduces their prices does not mean you have to jump on the band wagon and lower yours, avoid knee jerk reactions, and remain confident in prices you set for the quality of service you provide. Remember the saying "You get what you pay for". I had this happen many times to me and by sticking by my prices you will soon see that customers start coming to you in fear that a greatly reduced price by your competitors means less of a quality job is being done.

Be polite to your competitors; keep your friends close and your enemies closer. Who knows, maybe you can help each other out when the other is in a bind getting a job done; needing a part that is backordered and a customer just needs that reel now. There are more than enough customers out there to share.

You do not have to constantly monitor your competitors; if you are providing an honest, reliable service at a fair price then you will consistently have repeat customers. Too many new business owners believe everything is about price, when actually it's about quality of service. Would you be willing to pay a little bit more to have a reliable service that you can count on? Of course, and so would your customers. The key is, don't undersell yourself, know your expenses, and adjust your profit margin accordingly to what you are comfortable with.

Offer your customers a great service guarantee that will assure them if there is a problem later you will stand behind your service. I've seen a few repair shops go as far as to offer a lifetime guarantee on services; however I think this might be extreme, certainly it will generate large amounts of initial work but it will soon taper off as you are eliminating your repeat customers. A reasonable limit of time, of 60 days will more than enough assure your customer of quality work and will not lock you into a lifetime commitment for previous service.

When your business is first starting out it is important for you to know exactly what your competitors are offering their customers, and what they are not offering. By offering a few simple extra services that your competitors do not can quite often be just the thing that wins customers over to your business. But more often than not, simple business etiquette will impress your customers, such as returning phone calls or emails promptly, being courteous and polite, remembering to thank them for their business, and making each of your customers feel special to your business.

This may sound strange but what I have found works best with competitors is to get to know them, talk with them, let them know you are just starting up. You will be surprised how helpful they can be, and will usually gladly give you tips on what their customers love or don't love. After all, they will hear about your business sooner or later.

Sample Forms

REEL SERVICE DROP-OFF

This form is to be left at your drop-off locations for customers to fill out.

The Reel Mechanic
1212 Reel Way
Birmingham, AL 35565
205-555-1111

The Reel Mechanic will pickup reels every Tuesday and Friday of each week. If you need your reel serviced please feel out this form and leave your reel and this form with the cashier.

Name:
_____
_____

Address:
_____
_____

City, State, Zip Code:
_____

Phone Number:
_____

Number of Reels: _____

Brand: _____ Model: _____

Brand: _____ Model:
_____

Brand: _____ Model:
_____

Brand: _____ Model:
_____

Brand: _____ Model:
_____

Brand: _____ Model:
_____

What service do you need?
_____
_____
_____
____

REEL SERVICE PRICE LIST

This price sheet should also be left at your drop-off locations.

The Reel Mechanic
1212 Reel Way
Birmingham, AL 35565
205-555-1111

LABOR PRICES

$16.95 Per Freshwater Bait casting Reel
$14.95 Per Freshwater Spinning Reel
$34.95 Per Saltwater Lever Drag Reel
$36.95 Per Saltwater 2 Speed Lever Drag Reel
* includes cleaning and inspection, parts are not included.

If you have 3 or more reels we offer a 10% discount off labor.

If you have any question please call the number listed above.

Reel Service & Parts Directory

This reel service and parts supply directory will provide you with a list of reputable business that can provide parts for all your servicing needs. You can also visit us online at www.reelschematic.com

The Reel Doctor

Providing services and repairs for reels, rods, trolling motors, and underwater cameras
8732 – 51 Avenue
Edmonton, AB
T6E 5E8
Canada
Inside Canada – 1.866.431.0146
Outside Canada – 1.780.431.0146
service@reeldr.com
www.reeldr.com

Bucko's Tackle Service

Reel Parts and Service
191 Stafford Road
Fall River, MA 02721
1.508.674.7900
mjbucko@mindspring.com
www.buckosparts.com

JL Reel Service

Reel Parts and Service
910 N. Washington Avenue
Madison, SD 57042
605.256.4431
www.jlreelservice.com

Bay Area Reel Service

Reel Servicing and Repair
11201 Linden Lane
Port Richey, FL 34668
1.813.728.5865
www.bayareareelservice.com

Tom White Rod & Reel Repair

1024 New Scotland Road
Albany, New York 12208
1.518.488.9094
twhite10@nycap.rr.com
www.fishing-reel-repair.com

Mike's Reel Repair

#108-31060 Peardonville Road
Abbotsford, BC, Canada V2T6K5
1.888.404.1119
www.mikereelrepair.com

Dave's Reel Service
602 Avon Court
Vernon Hills, IL 60061
1.847.549.7170
repair@davesreelservice.com
www.davesreelservice.com

Anglers Parts Can
Large Supply of Reel Parts
Box 571
Sun Prairie, WI 53590
1.608.225.5501
www.anglerspartscan.com

Vintage Reels
The Old Reel Collectors Association (ORCA)
www.orcaonline.org

Warranty Service

Abu-Garcia Reels

Abu Garcia warrants to the original purchaser that its tackle products are free from defects in materials or workmanship for a period of one (1) year from the date of purchase. If a product proves defective in some way, return it prepaid and with proof of the date of purchase, to:

Abu Garcia /Pure Fishing
Attn: Angler Service
1900 18th Street Spirit Lake,
IA 51360

In the case of fishing rods please include $9.95 to cover return postage and handling. If after inspection, we determine that the product was defective in material or workmanship, we shall, at our option, repair or replace it without charge. We are not responsible for normal wear and tear, for equipment used commercially or for failures caused by accidents, abuse, alteration, modification, misuse or improper care.

There are no other express warranties beyond the terms of this limited warranty. In no event shall any implied warranties, including merchantability and fitness for a particular purpose, extend beyond the duration of the express warranty contained herein. In no event shall Berkley/Pure Fishing be liable for incidental or consequential damages.

Some states do not allow limitations on how long an implied warranty lasts or the exclusion of limitation of incidental or consequential damages, so the above limitations or exclusions may not apply to you. This warranty gives you specific rights and you may have other rights which vary from state to state.

Accurate Reels

How Long Does The Limited Warranty Coverage Last? This limited warranty runs for a period of five (5) years starting from the date that the ATD reel was first purchased by the consumer. Coverage terminates if you sell or otherwise transfer the reel.

What Does The Limited Warranty Cover? Accurate Fishing Products warrants to the original purchaser that its ATD fishing reels are free from defects in material and workmanship with the exceptions stated below. Accurate Fishing Products will also, free of charge, lubricate your ATD reel one (1) time per year during the term of this Limited Warranty.

What Is Not Covered By This Limited Warranty? This limited warranty does not cover damage or problems caused by misuse, abuse, neglect, accident, installation, alterations or failure to properly maintain the reel.

What Will Accurate Fishing Products Do? Accurate Fishing Products will repair or replace any reel which is defective in material or workmanship covered by this limited warranty at no charge. Accurate Fishing Products will also, free of charge, lubricate your ATD reel one (1) time per year during the term of this Limited Warranty.

How Do You Get Service? If something goes wrong

with your reel, or you want to receive the annual lubrication service, send it to Accurate Fishing Products, postage pre-paid, along with a sales receipt or other proof of the date of purchase. Be sure to include a short note explaining the problem.

Send the ATD reel to Accurate Fishing Products at:
Accurate Fishing Products
Warranty Repairs
807 E. Parkridge Avenue
Corona, California 92879
1-888-ACCU-372

Please pack your reel with all parts that have been removed securely in a sturdy box. Be certain that your package is adequately insured and mailed with a shipping company that has tracking capabilities. Be sure to include your name, address and telephone number. Accurate Fishing Products will inspect your reel and contact you within 30 days of receipt to inform you whether the problem is covered by this limited warranty. There is no charge for the inspection.

What Are The Warranty Limitations And Limitations Of Liability? There are no other express warranties. Any warranty of merchantability or fitness for a particular purpose is limited to the duration of this limited warranty. Accurate Fishing Products shall NOT be liable for any loss of use, loss of time, inconvenience, commercial loss, or other incidental or consequential damages. Some states do not allow limitations on how long an implied warranty lasts, or the exclusion or limitation of incidental or consequential damages, so the above limitations and exclusions may not apply to you. This limited warranty gives you specific legal rights, you may have additional rights which vary from state to state.

Avet Reels

Avet Reels one year Limited Warranty

Avet Reels, Inc. warrants to the original purchaser that this product will be free from defects in materials and workmanship for a period of one year from the date of purchase. This warranty does not cover damage or malfunctions caused by accident, abuse or normal expected wear. It will be considered VOID if the reel has been subjected to damage by the owner's failure to provide necessary maintenance. If your Avet reel has a defect within the terms of the warranty, you should return it to us, postage pre-paid, to:

Avet Reels, Inc.
9687 Topanga Cyn. Pl.
Chatsworth, CA 91311.

In addition, please provide a short explanation of

the problem you are experiencing with the product. We shall repair or replace the reel, at our option, without any further cost to you, including free return transportation. However, if the repair is not covered by the provisions of this warranty, Avet will perform the repair and return with a claim to you for labor, parts and return shipping charge.

All warranties which may be implied by operation of law, including, but not limited to, warranties of fitness for any particular purpose, shall be limited to one year from the date of purchase. In no event shall Avet Reels, Inc. be liable for incidental or consequential damages for breach of this warranty or any other warranty which may be implied by law. Some states do not allow limitations on how long an implied warranty lasts, and some states do not allow the exclusion of incidental or consequential damages, so the above limitation and/or exclusion may not apply to you.

This warranty gives you specific legal rights, and you may also have other rights which vary from state to state.

Daiwa Reels

Q. Where do I send my Daiwa rod and reel for repair and service?
A. You may send your reel to any of Daiwa's Authorized Warranty Centers or to our North American Service Center. Please check the following link for the nearest Daiwa Service Center. You must send your rod directly to our North American Service Center:

Daiwa Corporation
North American Service Center
12851 Midway Place
Cerritos, CA 90703
(562) 802-9589

Q. How do I file a warranty claim?
A. Daiwa will repair or replace without charge any Daiwa rod or reel which is defective in workmanship or materials within one year from the date of purchase by the consumer. Please retain your sales slip as proof of purchase date in the event warranty work becomes necessary. Please follow these instructions when returning rods or reels for warranty repair:

Do not remove parts

Enclose proof of purchase and a statement of warranty claim with nature of problem. Also, please list the model name and number of reel/rod and your return address.

To protect against loss or damage in transit, your reel/rod should be carefully packaged and adequately insured. Please retain all shipping receipts.

Q. How long does it normally take for repair?
A. The average turnaround time for warranty and chargeable repair once payment is received is approximately 3-5 working days. It may vary depending on seasonal demand.

Q. How much does a non-warranty repair cost and how do I pay for it?
A. In order to provide the cost of repair we must examine the product. Please follow these instructions when returning rods or reels for repair:

Do not remove parts

State the nature of the problem. Also, please list the model name and number of reel/rod, and your return address.

To protect against loss or damage in transit, your reel/rod should be carefully packaged and adequately insured. Please retain all shipping receipts.

Once we examine your rod or reel we will forward an estimate to you.

Q. How do I order parts for my Daiwa reel?
A. You can order parts on line, by phone, or by mail. You may pay by credit card, check or money order, or COD.

Fin-Nor Reels

It is the goal of W.C. Bradley Co./Zebco Holdings to provide you with the very best customer service possible. However, not all products previously manufactured under the name Fin-Nor will continue to be supported from either a new build or service stand point.

Items no longer supported are:
PRIMEO: 1000,2000,3000,4000
ESTIMA: ES50UL, ES100 - ES600
FIN-ITE: F201 - F304
FIN-NOR LITE: S50UL, S100 - S600
QUESTLITE: QL1000 - QL4000
QUESTLITE GOLD: QLG1000 - QLG4000
INSHORE: ISX2000 - ISX6000
STEEL RIVER: SR1000 - SR4000
TYCOON: TYS7-1 through TYS7-4, TYS5-100 through TYS5-400

The following products will be supported from a service standpoint. Service support on each of these items presents differing opportunities by model, thus we have developed item-specific service programs for each model in this list. Please contact us to learn more about the service program that is unique to your Fin-nor product.

Support programs ARE available on these products:
AHAB: 8A, 12A, 16A, 20A, LD12 - LD80-2
FIN-ITE/FIN-ITE II: 23CL - 1012
MEGA LITE: ML1000 - ML4000
BIG GAME TROLLING: 120FNSP, 120FNSTD, 120FTRI, 25FNA - 90FNA, 50FLN, 60WFNA, 75FNA

When returning your Fin-Nor product, the following information is required to process the service:
1. Provide your Name and Address, telephone, fax number or e-mail address.
2. Properly package the product so there is no further damage during shipping.
3. Insure the package and send it pre-paid to the Fin-Nor Repair Department. (No COD shipments will be accepted)
4. To expedite the repair, give a credit card number in your description letter.
5. Check or money order is also acceptable.
6. Any charges incurred will include freight charges.

All packages should be shipped to our facility:

Warranty Service

Fin-Nor Repair Department
6505 Tower Lane
Claremore, OK 74019-4429

NOTE: Repairs will be returned via UPS, unless other arrangements are made prior to shipment. We will not ship to a P.O. Box, please provide a UPS delivery address (street address).

Any repairs not paid for will be disposed of after 30 days from the date listed on the notification letter.

Hardy Reels

Original User Lifetime Warranty Information

All other non carbon-fibre rods and all reels manufactured by House of Hardy are covered by our Original User Lifetime Warranty against material or manufacturing defects. Our other products, excluding leaders, tippet material and other consumables, carry our original user warranty of 12 months from date of purchase. This warranty applies to products that have been used in the manner that was intended. It does not cover normal wear and tear, or apply to products that have been neglected, altered or abused in anyway, nor to any consequential loss, relating to any defect. This warranty is given in addition to your statutory rights.

Okuma Reels

http://www.okumafishingteam.com/misc/warranty.html

U.S.A. Contact Information
U.S. Head Office
OKUMA FISHING TACKLE CORP.
2310 E. Locust Court, Ontario CA 91761
Tel: 909-923-2828
Fax: 909-923-2909
1-800-GO-OKUMA, 1-800-466-5862

For **parts and service issues,** please contact:
service@okumafishing.com

Pinnacle Reels

WARRANTY AND SERVICE

Your Pinnacle/Silstar fishing product carries a limited warranty for a period of one year from the date of purchase against defects in workmanship and or materials.

During this period, Silstar Corporation of America, Inc. will perform repairs or
effect replacement, at its option. The warranty extends only to the original (Consumer) owner with valid proof of purchase. The Original warranty is non-transferable.

Purchaser should return defective rod and/or reel postage prepaid, insured with valid proof of purchase (indicating the date purchased) with $15.00 to cover return postage payable to Silstar Corporation of America, Inc. This warranty will be VOID if the rod or reel is found to have been subject to unauthorized alterations, abuse or damaged by failure to provide necessary and reasonable maintenance.

Retailers and wholesale outlets for Pinnacle products are NOT authorized to perform warranty repairs or exchange on behalf of Pinnacle/Silstar. Pinnacle / Silstar reels and rods not covered by warranty may be repaired at nominal charge provided these reels and rods are returned postage prepaid. We reserve the right to replace a discontinued model with a current comparable model of our choosing. This warranty gives you specific legal rights, and you may also have other rights which vary from state to state.

SHIPPING INSTRUCTIONS

All reels and rods sent in for repair or warranty service should be carefully packed and insured. Please include your name, return address, telephone number, E-mail address where you can be reached, **$15.00** check made to **Silstar Corporation**, Inc. to cover return postage, along with detailed information on the nature of the problem.

Send the Product to:

Pinnacle / Silstar Consumer Warranty & Service Center
3142 Platt Springs Rd.
Springdale, SC 29170

Phone : (888) 794-2221
Fax :   (803) 794-2252
Email :   service@pinnaclefishing.com

Penn Reels

Penn Limited Warranty: Penn Fishing Tackle Mfg. Co. warrants its Products to be free from defects in materials and workmanship for a period of one year from the date of purchase. This warranty does not cover damage or malfunctions caused by accident, abuse, or normal expected wear. If your Penn Product has a defect within the terms of the warranty you can return it to Old Inlet Bait and Tackle or Penn to be replaced or repaired. All shipping and insurance costs and transportation arrangements will be borne by you and are your responsibility. Penn will repair or replace the Product, at their option, without further cost to you (including free return transportation and insurance). If, however, the repair is not covered by the provisions of the warranty, your Penn Product will be repaired and returned to you at a reasonable charge for labor, parts and return transportation and insurance.

Carefully package and send your reels to:
FACTORY REPAIR SERVICE
PENN FISHING TACKLE
3028 W. HUNTING PARK AVE.
PHILADELPHIA, PA 19132

We recommend you send your reels to Penn via UPS

so that the shipment can be tracked and we can verify receipt of your goods.

Penn Information Form:
To facilitate the processing of your reels, please fill out a Penn Repair Information Form and include it with your shipment.

Include your name and address, and a way (or ways) for us to contact you, either by phone or email. Provide the best time to contact you, either at home or at work. You should include your credit card number, expiration date, name on card and type of card. This will help speed up your transaction. If you do not include your credit card information, we will contact you when your reels arrive at Penn, and get all necessary credit card information before we begin working on your reels.

CREDIT CARDS ONLY.

If you require an estimate, you must note this on the "special instructions" section of the repair form or in your correspondence. If you do not require an estimate and all of the required information is provided, your reel will be entered into our system and the following charges will be applied to your credit card once the repair is complete:

Quantum Reels

Quantum products are warranted for a period of one (1) year from **date of original retail purchase** against defects in workmanship and/or materials. Purchaser should return defective products postage prepaid, insured with proof of purchase direct to Quantum at 6105 E. Apache, Tulsa, OK 74115. Quantum will repair or replace products at its option and return direct to purchaser.

This warranty does not cover Quantum products damaged due to abuse, misuse, normal wear, or excessive wear caused by neglect of cleaning and lubrication required or general service requirements due to owner's failure to provide reasonable and necessary maintenance.

Quantum products not covered by the Quantum Limited Warranty may be repaired at a nominal charge to the purchaser, provided parts are available and the product is returned with return postage prepaid.

"ALL INCIDENTAL AND/OR CONSEQUENTIAL DAMAGES ARE EXCLUDED FROM THIS WARRANTY INSERT. IMPLIED WARRANTIES ARE LIMITED TO THE LIFE OF THIS WARRANTY. SOME STATES DO NOT ALLOW LIMITATIONS ON HOW LONG AN IMPLIED WARRANTY LASTS OR THE EXCLUSION OR LIMITATION OF INCIDENTAL OR

CONSEQUENTIAL DAMAGES, SO THE ABOVE LIMITATIONS OR EXCLUSIONS MAY NOT APPLY TO YOU. THIS WARRANTY GIVES YOU SPECIFIC LEGAL RIGHTS, AND YOU MAY ALSO HAVE OTHER LEGAL RIGHTS WHICH MAY VARY FROM STATE TO STATE."

The warranties described herein shall be the sole and exclusive warranties granted by Quantum and shall be the sole and exclusive remedy available to the purchaser. Correction of defects, in the manner and time period described herein, shall constitute complete fulfillment of all liabilities and responsibilities of Quantum to the purchaser with regard to this product, and shall constitute full satisfaction of all claims, whether based on contract, negligence, strict liability or otherwise. Quantum shall not be liable or in any way responsible for any damages or defects caused by repairs or attempted repairs performed by anyone other than an authorized servicer. Nor shall Quantum be liable, or in any way responsible, for any incidental or consequential property damage. Quantum reserves the right to amend or change this warranty at any time.

THIS WARRANTY GIVES YOU SPECIFIC LEGAL RIGHTS, AND YOU MAY ALSO HAVE OTHER LEGAL RIGHTS WHICH MAY VARY FROM STATE TO STATE.

The provisions of this Warranty are in addition to, and not a modification of, or a subtraction from, the statutory warranties and other rights and remedies contained in any applicable legislation. To the extent that any provision of this Warranty is inconsistent with any applicable law, such provision shall be deemed voided or amended as necessary, to comply with such law.

Shakespeare

Your new Shakespeare product comes with a limited warranty for a period of one year against defects in material and/or workmanship. Shakespeare will have no other obligation and will not be liable for incidental or consequential damages. Shakespeare makes no implied warranty of MERCHANTABILITY OR FITNESS for any period beyond the duration of each limited warranty. This warranty does not cover damage caused by addition to or alteration of the product, accident, abuse or normal wear. This warranty does not extend to products, which are put to commercial or rental use.

Some state laws do not allow exclusion of incidental or consequential damages or limitation of the duration of implied warranties, so the above exclusion and limitations might not apply to you. This warranty gives you specific rights, which vary, from state to state.

Parts & Repair
The decision to repair or replace reels under warranty will be made by the Service Center. Rods under warranty will always be replaced. Shakespeare Service Center no longer repairs any fishing rods. Shakespeare reel which are no longer covered by warranty may be repaired at a nominal charge plus shipping and handling. Call the service center for details.

Old reels

Shakespeare has been in business for more than one hundred years. We retain parts and schematics for all reels that are six years old or less. Occasionally we may have parts for older models. Please call the Service Center for more information.

Instructions for Warranty Service

Send rods, freight prepaid and insured, to the Shakespeare Service Center at 3801 Westmore Drive Columbia SC 29223 , along with a note stating how the item was broken or damaged. Include name, mailing address, phone number, proof of date of purchase, and $7.50 for return postage and handling. For one piece rods 6'6" or longer, include an additional $2.50 for oversize fee.

Send reels, freight prepaid and insured, to the Shakespeare Service Center, along with a note stating how the item was broken or damaged. Include name, mailing address, phone number, proof of date of purchase, and $6.50 for return postage and handling.

Shakespeare will repair or replace the product at its option and return directly to the purchaser.

All authorized repairs are made by the Shakespeare Service Center in Columbia, SC. Canadian customers contact:

Warranty Service

Rockey's Tackle Repair
10 Brammer Drive
Orillia, Ontario L3V 7T4
Canada
705-325-3526

Shimano Reels

Shimano warrants to the original purchaser that this product will be free from non-conformities in material or workmanship for the period of one year from the date of purchase.

To request repairs (or non-warranty service) send your reel, postage pre-paid, to the Shimano Authorized Warranty Center nearest you. Retailers and wholesale outlets are not required or authorized to perform warranty repairs or exchanges on behalf of Shimano. If sending your reel to Shimano directly, please call for verification on due date as some seasons experience high volume.

All warranty requests must be accompanied by a dated sales receipt, your name, address, telephone number (daytime), email address (optional), and a brief description of the issues related to your warranty request.

The following items will not be covered under warranty:
Non- ARB Ball Bearings, Roller Bearings

Zebco Reels

Zebco products are warranted for a period of one (1) year from date of original retail purchase against defects in workmanship and/or materials. Purchaser should return defective products postage prepaid, insured with proof of purchase direct to Zebco at 6105 E. Apache, Tulsa, OK 74115. Zebco will repair or replace products at its option and return direct to purchaser.

This warranty does not cover Zebco products damaged due to abuse, misuse, normal wear, or excessive wear caused by neglect of cleaning and lubrication required or general service requirements due to owner's failure to provide reasonable and necessary maintenance.

Zebco products not covered by the Zebco Limited Warranty may be repaired at a nominal charge to the purchaser, provided parts are available and the product is returned with return postage prepaid.

"ALL INCIDENTAL AND/OR CONSEQUENTIAL DAMAGES ARE EXCLUDED FROM THIS WARRANTY INSERT. IMPLIED WARRANTIES ARE LIMITED TO THE LIFE OF THIS WARRANTY. SOME STATES DO NOT ALLOW LIMITATIONS ON HOW LONG AN IMPLIED WARRANTY LASTS OR THE EXCLUSION OR LIMITATION OF INCIDENTAL OR CONSEQUENTIAL DAMAGES, SO THE ABOVE LIMITATIONS OR EXCLUSIONS MAY NOT APPLY

TO YOU. THIS WARRANTY GIVES YOU SPECIFIC LEGAL RIGHTS, AND YOU MAY ALSO HAVE OTHER LEGAL RIGHTS WHICH MAY VARY FROM STATE TO STATE."

The warranties described herein shall be the sole and exclusive warranties granted by Zebco and shall be the sole and exclusive remedy available to the purchaser. Correction of defects, in the manner and time period described herein, shall constitute complete fulfillment of all liabilities and responsibilities of Zebco to the purchaser with regard to this product, and shall constitute full satisfaction of all claims, whether based on contract, negligence, strict liability or otherwise. Zebco shall not be liable or in any way responsible for any damages or defects caused by repairs or attempted repairs performed by anyone other than an authorized servicer. Nor shall Zebco be liable, or in any way responsible, for any incidental or consequential property damage. Zebco reserves the right to amend or change this warranty at any time.

THIS WARRANTY GIVES YOU SPECIFIC LEGAL RIGHTS, AND YOU MAY ALSO HAVE OTHER LEGAL RIGHTS WHICH MAY VARY FROM STATE TO STATE.

The provisions of this Warranty are in addition to, and not a modification of, or a subtraction from, the statutory warranties and other rights and remedies contained in any applicable legislation. To the extent that any provision of this Warranty is inconsistent with any applicable law, such provision shall be deemed voided or amended as necessary, to comply with such law.

A

Abu-Garcia Reels, 100
Accountants, 1, 25
Accurate Reels, 102
Advertising, 2, 77, 78, 85
Adwords, 2, 82
aluminum, 59
Avet Reels, 104, 105

B

Ball Bearings, 121
Bank Accounts, 1, 22
Business License, 20, 21
business name, 7, 8, 9, 10, 11, 12, 13, 48, 50, 79

C

COMPETITORS, 2, 90
Corporations, 14
CPAs, 25
Credit Cards, 1, 22, 24
CTR, 86
Customer Records, 1, 37

D

Daiwa, 67, 71, 106
Domain Names, 48
drag, 61, 68, 69

E

EIN, 13, 14, 15, 17, 18, 19, 20
Email, 1, 2, 49, 79, 113
Employees, 1, 16, 36

Estates, 19

F

fictitious business name, 8, 11, 12
Fin-Nor Reels, 108
foot traffic, 4

G

graphite, 68, 72
Graphite, 65

H

Hardy Reels, 110
Home Office, 1, 2

I

Image Tags, 1, 55
Internet, 4, 5, 7, 20, 29, 30, 31, 43, 49, 55, 78, 82

K

keywords, 53, 54, 56, 82, 84, 85

L

Leased Property, 1, 2
Link Titles, 1, 55
LLC, 16, 17, 18, 19
Lubrication, 63, 67, 68, 70, 71, 72

M

Marketing, 2, 30, 77, 79

Meta Tags, 52
Molybdenum Disulfide, 65

O

Okuma, 111

P

PARTNERSHIPS, 12
Penn, 32, 114, 115
pinion, 68, 69
Pinnacle Reels, 112
Pricing, 1, 33, 56

Q

Quantum Reels, 116

R

ReelSchematic Chile Pepper Sauce, 32, 63
ReelSchematic Muscle Grease, 32, 63

S

Sales Tax, 20

SEO, 44, 56
Shakespeare, 119
Shimano Reels, 121
Sole Proprietors, 14
stainless steel, 59, 61
store front, 8
Super Slick, 32, 64, 66

T

Trusts, 19
Tungsten Disulfide, 64, 65, 66

V

Vendor Records, 1, 39
Viscosity, 64

W

website, 7, 34, 43, 44, 45, 49, 51, 53, 54, 79, 85
Website Hosting, 48

Z

Zebco Reels, 122

NOTES:

NOTES:

Made in the USA
Charleston, SC
12 January 2010